MARY'S
Journey

MARY'S Journey

Louis J. Cameli

Foreword by
Francis Cardinal George, O.M.I.

Christian Classics™

Allen, Texas

NIHIL OBSTAT:
Rev. Msgr. Glenn D. Gardner, J.C.D.
Censor Librorum

IMPRIMATUR:
† Most Rev. Charles V. Grahmann
Bishop of Dallas

February 24, 2003

The Nihil Obstat and Imprimatur are official declarations that the material reviewed is free of doctrinal or moral error. No implication is contained therein that those granting the Nihil Obstat and Imprimatur agree with the contents, opinions, or statements expressed.

Acknowledgments

The Scripture quotations contained herein are from the *New Revised Standard Version Bible: Catholic Edition,* copyright © 1993 and 1989 by the Division of Christian Education for the National Council of the Churches of Christ in the U.S.A. Used by permission. All rights reserved.

Send all inquiries to:
Christian Classics
An RCL Company
200 East Bethany Drive
Allen, Texas 75002-3804

Telephone: 800-264-0368 / 972-390-6400
Fax: 800-688-8356 / 972-390-6560

E-mail: cservice@rcl-enterprises.com

Website: **www.ThomasMore.com**

Printed in the United States of America

Library of Congress Control Number: 2003102132

6845   ISBN 0-87061-228-X

1 2 3 4 5   07 06 05 04 03

TO THE MEMORY OF MY MOTHER

LENA MASSI CAMELI

1926–1986

MULIER FORTIS FIDELIS
NECNON SAPIENS

CONTENTS

Foreword

Introduction

PART ONE: Mary, Woman of Faith 13

The Things and Times 17

Origins 19

Growing Up 21

Openness 24

The Call of God 27

Experience of Accepting God's Call 33

Service: Expression of the Call 36

Traveling with Joseph to Bethlehem 38

The Birth of Jesus 42

In the Temple 46

At Nazareth 51

The Beginning of Jesus' Ministry 56

Observing the Ministry of Jesus 62

The Suffering and Death of Jesus 68

The Resurrection of Jesus 72

The Coming of the Holy Spirit 77

PART TWO: The Church's Journey of Faith with Mary 79

The Church's Journey of Faith with Mary 81

Marian Doctrines 85

Mary, the Mother of God 87

Mary, the Virgin Mother of Jesus Christ 99

CONTENTS

Foreword 9

Introduction 11

PART ONE: Mary's Journey of Faith 13

The Hinge and Link 15

Origins 19

Growing Up 21

Openness 24

The Call of God 27

The Cost of Accepting God's Call 31

Service: Expression of the Call 35

Traveling with Joseph to Bethlehem 38

The Birth of Jesus 42

In the Temple 46

At Nazareth 51

The Beginning of Jesus' Ministry 56

Observing the Ministry of Jesus 63

The Suffering and Death of Jesus 68

The Resurrection of Jesus 72

The Coming of the Holy Spirit 77

PART TWO: The Church's Journey of Faith with Mary . . . 79

The Church's Journey of Faith with Mary 81

Marian Doctrines 85

Mary, the Mother of God 87

Mary, the Virgin Mother of Jesus Christ 92

The Immaculate Conception 95

The Assumption. 100

Marian Devotion 104

The Communion of Saints 104

Mary's Intercession 106

Devotion and Devotions 110

Apparitions of Mary 115

The Imitation of Mary: Mary as a Model 119

Possibilities for Everyone Who Believes 120

Possibilities for People in Particular Circumstances . 121

PART THREE: The Church Celebrates the Feasts of Mary . 123

The Church Celebrates the Feasts of Mary 125

The Immaculate Conception: December 8 130

Our Lady of Guadalupe,
    Patroness of the Americas: December 12 . . . 134

Mary, the Mother of God: January 1 141

The Annunciation: March 25 145

The Visitation: May 31 149

The Assumption: August 15 153

The Birth of Mary: September 8 156

Concluding Meditation 160

A Selection of Marian Prayers 163

Bibliography 173

Scripture Index 175

FOREWORD

To be a Catholic is to be devoted to Mary. Indeed, most people who call themselves Christians recognize Mary as an actor in God's plan of salvation for the world and value their relationship with her. The Church's living Tradition, rooted in the Gospels and in the life of the young Church at Jerusalem, puts us in touch with Mary. She is inextricably part of the story of God's intervention in the human situation to heal and to transform. Led unfailingly by the Holy Spirit, in her teaching and practice, the Church over twenty centuries has developed these truths and insights into a rich heritage of appreciation of Mary's continuing role in the lives of followers of her divine Son. All that Mary means to us is founded on the fact that Mary is the Mother of God made man and therefore also Mother of the body of Christ, which is the Church.

This has practical implications for the living of a Christian life:

◆ We venerate Mary—we have devotion to her as a principal icon of God's love and presence with his people; we express this in prayer and religious sentiments.

◆ We imitate Mary—her example is a deeply attractive and sure guide in the following of Christ.

◆ We seek Mary's intercession on our behalf—she is our advocate with her Son; every need, even the most mundane, can be the object of the requests we make as we solicit her prayers.

In this book on Mary's journey, Father Louis Cameli helps us to reflect on certain aspects of the part Mary plays in the story of God's gracious dealings with us—her role in God's plan to save us from sin and let us share in the supernatural life of grace; her substantial and continuing part in the mission and ministry of Jesus and his Church. I believe that, with his felicitous and easily grasped explanations, Father Cameli brings fresh light to key doctrinal issues concerning Mary— the truth that Mary is Mother of God, her virginal conception of Jesus, and her immaculate conception.

It is my hope that many will find new depth in their devotion to Mary and new confidence in her intercession by reading this book. Pastors will be grateful for the help it can give them for a prayerful preparation of their homilies. Father Cameli's deep faith and his love of the Church shape his words and judgments.

May the great Mother of God cast her mantle of loving care anew over the Church; may she reward the author of this book who has written well of her.

—Francis Cardinal George, O.M.I.
Archbishop of Chicago

INTRODUCTION

The Discovery of a Journey

 mages, especially images from infancy and child-hood, burn themselves into one's memory. "The first time I saw. . ." speaks of a privileged moment, a special time—whatever it was that was seen.

The first time I saw an image of the Blessed Virgin Mary was very early in my life. I think I was in my bedroom, and my mother showed me a picture in a book, a picture of Mary. She appeared to be a kind and caring woman. Then my mother taught me a short prayer calling on Mary's help. The memory stays with me.

Something similar happened in the Church. From the very beginning, the Church caught sight of an image of Mary. She was full of grace, the Lord was with her; she was blessed among women, and blessed was the fruit of her womb, Jesus. That early image of Mary made a deep and lasting impression on the memory of the Church.

Although the earliest images of special people in our lives remain, we know that when we return to them the images have gaps. We return throughout our lives to fill in the picture, make it more complete, and thus appreciate the person even more. *Mary's Journey* is the result of my attempt to fill in my picture of Mary. It is a meditation on Mary in the Bible, in the teachings of the Church, and in our life of worship and devotion.

I follow a pattern similar to one set by Pope John Paul II in his encyclical letter *Redemptoris Mater* (*On the Blessed Virgin Mary in the Life of the Pilgrim Church*, 1987). He introduced his letter saying, "I wish to consider primarily that 'pilgrimage of faith' in which 'the Blessed Virgin advanced'. . . (It) is not just a question of the Virgin Mother's life story, of her personal journey of faith . . . it is also a question of the history of the whole People of God, of all those who take part in the same 'pilgrimage of faith' " (5).

I invite you to share in this meditation. Together we will certainly recognize the unique and privileged place of Mary in the story of salvation and in the Church. We will also see her setting a pattern for our journey and accompanying us along the way. My hope is that you, the reader, will return to your own image of Mary, the Mother of God, and find her more alive and present to you than ever before.

The catechetical project represented by *Mary's Journey* spans nearly twenty-five years. I am grateful to so many people along the way who have helped, encouraged, and supported this project: Father Candido Pozo, S.J., my teacher of Mariology at the Gregorian University; my students at Mundelein Seminary who studied and meditated with me; the late Monsignor Eugene Bilski who as director of the National Shrine of the Immaculate Conception initiated and directed the project; the staff of W.H. Sadlier, Inc., which published the first edition; the staff of Thomas More, publisher of this new and revised edition. Finally, special thanks to my bishop, Cardinal Francis George, O.M.I., who has encouraged and supported the revision and republishing of *Mary's Journey*.

The return to our image of Mary cannot and will not end with this book. Our return to Mary will continue, because our journey of faith continues. These pages, I hope, will serve you well, at least for this part of your journey.

—Father Louis J. Cameli
Director of Ongoing Formation for Priests,
Archdiocese of Chicago

PART ONE

Mary's Journey of Faith

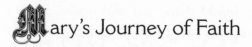

Mary's Journey of Faith

The Hinge and Link

Origins

Growing Up

Openness

The Call of God

The Cost of Accepting God's Call

Service: Expression of the Call

Traveling with Joseph to Bethlehem

The Birth of Jesus

In the Temple

At Nazareth

The Beginning of Jesus' Ministry

Observing the Ministry of Jesus

The Suffering and Death of Jesus

The Resurrection of Jesus

The Coming of the Holy Spirit

"The Holy Spirit led the Second Vatican Council to describe our Lady's life on earth as a pilgrimage of faith. This approach to the Virgin Mary based on the Bible is especially suited to the needs of our day."

Pastoral Letter, *Behold Your Mother,* 12

The Hinge and Link

Not so long ago, I was shopping in a local discount department store. As I walked down one of the aisles, I overheard a mother and daughter talking with one of the salesclerks. It was a special kind of exchange, one that you could describe as "made in America." The mother and daughter appeared to be Mexican Americans. The daughter was about ten or eleven, with jet-black hair that framed a beautiful oval face the color of very light cocoa. She was translating her mother's rapid-fire Spanish into clear and exact Midwestern American English. With equal ease, she digested the clerk's instructions for using an electric can opener and translated them for her mother into fluent Spanish. It was a scene that is fairly common around Chicago, and it stirred up a number of thoughts for me.

I thought of my mother and grandmother doing the very same thing not so long ago. I recalled the courage of my immigrant grandparents as they left their home for a land of promise for themselves and their children. Most of all, I thought of my mother and her generation, the first generation born in this land of promise. Like the little girl in the store, my mother was a hinge between the Old World and the New, between two languages, between the promise and the fulfillment. Much is asked of the child of immigrant parents, much more than simply knowing two different languages. The child must know and understand at least partially the hopes and dreams of the parents as well as the ways of the "old" world that they have brought with them. The child must also grasp the complicated ways of the "new" and foreign world. Then that child can link and bridge the world of dreams and promise with the world of fulfillment, where the dreams can become reality.

To be the hinge or link between worlds and generations is obviously no easy task, yet it is important and necessary. All of us who trace our origins to immigrants find ourselves indebted to the dreams and courage of those who left their homes to build a better life in America. But we are also indebted in a special way to the generation, the firstborn in this country, who linked the Old World and the New.

As we trace Mary's journey of faith, it may be helpful to recall the image of immigrant children as a hinge and link. And before we discuss anything about Mary, we should note her place in the Bible and in history, where she stands at the center as a hinge and link. Mary appears at the end of the Old Testament, the Hebrew Scriptures, which tell the story of how God chose the people of Israel, made a covenant with them, and promised them a future beyond their dreams. She appears at the beginning of the New Testament, which tells the story of God's faithfulness to the promise and its fulfillment in Jesus Christ.

Mary's journey begins at the intersection of promise and fulfillment. Very much like the children of immigrants, she takes on the whole story of her people, with its struggles and frustrations, with its triumphs and joys, and—most of all—with its dream and its promise. The story of Mary's people, the people of Israel, begins with Abraham, with whom God made a covenant and promise saying: "As for me, this is my covenant with you: You shall be the ancestor of a multitude of nations. . . . I will establish my covenant between me and you, and your offspring after you throughout their generations, for an everlasting covenant, to be God to you and to your offspring after you" (Genesis 17:4, 7). Mary draws together the story of that covenant which began with Abraham and continued with Moses and the prophets. She is the memory of her people, the one who holds and treasures God's promise and faithfulness when she sings in her song of praise, the *Magnificat:* "He has helped his servant Israel, in remembrance of his mercy, according to the promise he made to our ancestors, to Abraham and to his descendants forever" (Luke 1:54–55).

Mary also stands before the fulfillment of the promise and the dream. She is the mother of Jesus, who is the fulfillment and completion of the promise. He is in himself the new and everlasting covenant. Saint Paul wrote, "For in him every one of God's promises is a 'Yes.' For this reason it is through him that we say the 'Amen,' to the glory of God" (2 Corinthians 1:20). She is really, truly a link and a hinge between promise and fulfillment.

Mary, as we have said, begins her journey of faith at the intersection of promise and fulfillment. This is her position in the story of God's love for the human family as it comes alive in the people of Israel and finds fulfillment in Jesus Christ. Although Mary's journey of faith and her position are unique to her, there are ways in which we can identify our own journey of faith with hers. We ourselves live in an in-between time. Whenever we experience our brokenness healed, whenever we come alive in new and generous ways because God's love has touched us through other people, we catch a glimpse of the new life and the fulfillment of our deepest desires in Jesus Christ. In the words of the Second Vatican Council, we know that "the promised restoration which we are awaiting has already begun in Christ" (*Dogmatic Constitution on the Church*, 48). Still, there is a brokenness about our lives; the love we give and receive is not perfect. These are signs that we still live on the edge of the promise. As a community of believers in the Church, as people who believe, pray, and serve together, we can come to understand ourselves and our journey of faith. We recognize that our journey of faith proceeds between promise and fulfillment. In fact, we are the link and the hinge between the reign of God that has begun in Jesus and the reign of God that must still take hold of our lives completely.

Origins

The 1981 Oscar for best film went to *Ordinary People,* the story of a family trying to cope with the death of a son. Although it dealt with the highly charged emotional issues of life and death and parent-child relationships, it was not the story itself that made the film a success. Rather, *Ordinary People* was successful because it uncovered the ordinary and yet dramatic character of our own lives, a fact that we are aware of but find difficult to express. Most of us think that if our lives are not in public view, if there is no big name attached to them, they are undramatic—perhaps not even very important. In its own way, *Ordinary People* alerted us to that prejudice and told our story. That is why, I believe, it has had such a gripping effect on its viewers.

As we trace Mary's journey of faith, we ought to keep in mind the image of ordinary people—especially when we reflect on her origins. The Bible maintains a complete silence about the birth of Mary and her family. A lively curiosity and interest in those details led to the development of stories that filled in some of the missing information; gospel-like accounts were collected at the beginning of the second century. In one of them, Mary's parents were given the names Anna and Joachim. Although the accounts seem to have originated more in the popular imagination than in accurate reporting, they have exercised influence throughout the centuries.

The Bible, as we just mentioned, maintains a complete silence about the birth of Mary and about her family. Even so, the silence of the Bible says something about Mary's origin—that it was hidden and ordinary. In fact, although that may not seem to be much information, it tells us a great deal. She was born, like the majority of us, in relative obscurity. Like us also, she was born to ordinary parents. In other words, she was like us.

Mary's journey of faith, then, started from a point that was hidden and ordinary, and much of her life followed that same path. This is not to say that it was unimportant. This is precisely the prejudice that the movie *Ordinary People* uncovered. In ordinariness and hiddenness, the drama of Mary's journey of faith began and unfolded. Realizing this can help us link our own journey of faith with hers. Like Mary's journey, ours is also ordinary and hidden. This is not a new understanding, but one that needs to be called to mind frequently. Saint Paul reminded the Colossians of this when he wrote, "Your life is hidden with Christ in God" (Colossians 3:3).

Surprisingly, the silence of the Bible about Mary's origins reveals far more than it hides. The silence tells us that the origins of her journey, as well as our own, can only be found in what is hidden and ordinary. Interestingly, one of the major lines of spiritual renewal over the last one hundred years has been a recovery of the sense of hiddenness and ordinariness in the journey of faith. In her autobiography, Saint Thérèse of Lisieux opened the eyes of many people with her "little way," that is, finding God in the ordinary events and relationships of life. Charles de Foucauld, a French priest and missionary of the Sahara, and his followers rediscovered "desert spirituality," a way of finding God in hiddenness, a way that we will consider in more detail when we reflect on Nazareth.

Growing Up

P arents want their children to grow up. Even more, they would like some formula or perhaps some technique to make sure that their children grow up perfectly. Of course, there is no special formula and no magic technique to make this happen. The growth of children, like the growth of plants and all living things, cannot be forced. The best that we can do is to provide a climate and environment in which development takes place. We can offer a loving home and nutritious food to children, just as we provide sunlight and water for plants. But these things do not make growth happen; they only support and favor the process.

The young Mary grew, just as her son Jesus grew. About the early years of Jesus, Scripture says: "The child grew and became strong, filled with wisdom; and the favor of God was upon him" (Luke 2:40); but about the early years of Mary, the Bible is silent. We therefore do not have an exact picture of her early journey of faith, how she fostered her faith relationship with God. What we do have, however, is a very clear picture of the climate and environment that supported and favored her growth in the journey of faith. We know this climate and environment because it was the faith of the people of Israel. We have already seen that Mary lived in the covenant faith of Israel, linking the promise with fulfillment. Now, we need to explore this covenant faith in more detail in order to understand how it provided Mary with a climate and environment for her growth.

Covenant faith has its roots in the pact, or agreement, that God made with the people of Israel. The very first quality of covenant faith is a sense of the closeness of God to his people and of the people to their God. This sense finds expression in a phrase that is repeated many times in the Old Testament: "You shall be my people, and I will be your God" (Ezekiel 36:28). Contained in this sense of mutual closeness is the experience of being a chosen people, of being specially called—a theme that runs through the book of Deuteronomy. The covenant faith—a trusting faith in God based on Israel's pact with God that made them the chosen people—supported and sustained Mary's development.

Although the Bible is silent about the prayer of Mary, we only have to look to the book of Psalms to find her prayer book. The Psalms, the prayers of the people of Israel, speak the mind and the heart of a people who feel a closeness to God, a sense of being chosen, and a trusting faith. The Psalms offer prayers for various occasions and moods. If Mary wanted to share with God her sense of trust, she might have turned to Psalm 62: "For God alone my soul waits in silence, for my hope is from him. He alone is my rock and my salvation, my fortress; I shall not be shaken" (Psalm 62:5–6). If she wanted enlightenment when life seemed confusing, she might have prayed: "Make me to know your ways, O LORD; teach me your paths" (Psalm 25:4). If she needed help, she would pray with open hands: "Hear the voice of my supplication, as I cry to you for help, as I lift up my hands toward your most holy sanctuary" (Psalm 28:2). One of her prayers of praise and thanksgiving was undoubtedly Psalm 136: "O give thanks to the LORD, for he is good, for his steadfast love endures forever" (Psalm 136:1).

The process of growing begins when good seed falls on good ground, not on the footpaths, not on rocks, and not among thorns. The environment and climate are critical for the process. Although we have few details about the years when Mary was growing up, we have considerable knowledge about the climate and environment of her faith. It was the faith of Israel in God's covenant, a faith that speaks out in the prayers of the Psalms. We can easily relate with Mary's journey of faith. We recognize that our own development in faith is not and cannot be forced. At the same time, we know how important it is to be in a climate and environment of faith-filled living. We belong to a church, a community of believing, praying, and serving disciples of Jesus. There we find the climate and environment in which we grow and move forward in our own journey of faith.

Openness

Nothing short-circuits a relationship more quickly than seeking to impose on and control the other person. Marriage counselors, for example, frequently hear complaints about imposition and control. "He wants to run my life," she says. And he says, "She won't bend a bit." Attitudes of imposition and control poison a relationship because they strike at freedom, the heart of a relationship. A relationship thrives when people are free to be themselves and, as free people, join themselves to each other to make one life out of two. Only then can they experience a whole new set of possibilities that come not from their individual lives but from their life together. Imposition and control cut out the rich possibilities enjoyed by two free individuals working together.

More positively, openness and availability are the attitudes needed for the growth and development of a relationship. Openness does not mean a passive do-whatever-you-want-to attitude. It takes work to be open. Openness never happens without opening, and this means clearing a path and removing obstacles. We need to remove from our lives whatever closes us, such as prejudices and past hurts and well-entrenched ways of doing things. Availability does not mean just being around. It, too, takes work. Availability means making ourselves present to others; physically, of course, but also in other less tangible ways: through letters or phone calls or gifts, or even in our thoughts. When we have worked at it and are truly open and available to another person, then we can let that person be free. The freedom that we share and brings us together will flower in a number of possibilities that would have been impossible for each person alone.

In the Bible, the process of becoming open and available is called *conversion*. In its root sense, the word means "change of heart." The change is a movement from being closed to being open, from being removed to being available and present. We have often heard the phrase "converted sinner." It indicates the making open and available of someone who was closed and removed because of the obstacle we call sin. Whatever the obstacle, resistance, or blockage, a person of faith needs a change of heart. Openness and availability allow us to enter into a relationship with God, to share a life together with new and countless and surprising possibilities. God, after all, can only move in an open heart.

Mary's journey of faith involved a commitment to make herself open and available to God. The proof of this comes from "reading backward" in her life, projecting back to the spiritual assumptions that underpin her life. So, her acceptance of God's call at the annunciation—"Here am I, the servant of the Lord; let it be with me according to your word" (Luke 1:38)—indicates what must have been her preparation for that momentous decision. In her way, she took up the call of the Old Testament prophet Isaiah, and of John the Baptist, who stands at the head of Mark's gospel: "See, I am sending my messenger ahead of you, who will prepare your way; the voice of one crying out in the wilderness: 'Prepare the way of the Lord, make his paths straight' " (Mark 1:2).

We can identify with Mary. Our identification may not be with the complete openness and availability that belonged uniquely to her, however. Rather, it will be with the process by which she opened herself to the Lord, making herself available to the possibilities of life with God. The gospel invites us to leave sin behind because sin obstructs the path to God and God's path to us. We hear the words of Jesus in the Sermon on the Mount: "Do not worry about your life, what you will eat or what you will drink, or about your body, what you will wear. Is not life more than food, and the body more than clothing?" (Matthew 6:25). We hear these words and know how our worries and cares can sometimes remove us from the sense of God's presence, how they make us remote and unavailable. Our own journey of faith, then, requires the same movement that marked Mary's journey—making ourselves open and available. The details will vary for each one of us, but we must sort through our own clutter—whatever can close us off from God and eventually cut off the possibilities of life with him.

The Call of God

A t the moment when the birth of Jesus is announced, we find the Bible's first reference to Mary's journey of faith. The story is taken from Luke's gospel: "In the sixth month the angel Gabriel was sent by God to a town in Galilee called Nazareth, to a virgin engaged to a man whose name was Joseph, of the house of David. The virgin's name was Mary. And he came to her and said, 'Greetings, favored one! The Lord is with you.' But she was much perplexed by his words and pondered what sort of greeting this might be. The angel said to her, 'Do not be afraid, Mary, for you have found favor with God. And now, you will conceive in your womb and bear a son, and you will name him Jesus. He will be great, and will be called the Son of the most High, and the Lord God will give to him the throne of his ancestor David. He will reign over the house of Jacob forever, and of his kingdom there will be no end.' Mary said to the angel, 'How can this be, since I am a virgin?' The angel said to her, 'The Holy Spirit will come upon you, and the power of the Most High will overshadow you; therefore the child to be born will be holy; he will be called Son of God. And now, your relative Elizabeth in her old age has also conceived a son; and this is the sixth month for her who was said to be barren. For nothing will be impossible with God.' Then Mary said, 'Here am I, the servant of the Lord; let it be with me according to your word.' Then the angel departed from her" (Luke 1:26–38).

The traditional name for this story is the *annunciation*. An angel, or heavenly messenger, made the announcement. The focus of the passage is on the Messiah, the Word made flesh, who came to dwell among us. Still, from the viewpoint of Mary's journey of faith, the passage also tells the story of her call to be the mother of the Messiah. It tells us that she was both surprised and overwhelmed by the call she received. We can easily identify with her emotions. For many people, the great moment of call and invitation comes when they hear the words, "I love you. Will you share your life with me?" Even if people have known each other for a long time, there is an element of surprise. They may also feel overwhelmed, as well as happy and afraid—all at the same time. No one enters our life in a deep and significant way and leaves us feeling neutral, especially if it involves an offer of a new life. Mary's reaction rings true. It is the kind of reaction we can imagine in ourselves.

The style and tone of the exchange between Mary and the angel show another side of the story. The angel invites her, calls on her freedom. There is no imposition, no blind fate involved. Mary senses a call that recognizes her freedom, and she responds out of her freedom. If we dwell on Mary's experience of freedom, we can come to understand this decisive moment in her journey of faith, as well as the way that God moves in our own lives.

As we saw earlier, the loving and close relationships we have with one another must involve freedom. If two people love each other genuinely, they let each other be; not because they are indifferent and do not care, but because the greatest gift they can give is the freedom to be themselves. When friends try to reshape each other according to their own image and likeness, the end of the friendship is not far away.

When they value the uniqueness of each other, they develop bonds that cannot be broken easily.

At the same time, when people truly love each other, they want to conform freely to the will of the one who is loved. When people love each other, there is no contradiction between being free and conforming to each other's will. This was Mary's experience in her call. She had known the love of God—God's love for her and her love for God. She heard the call and the invitation. She freely responded and accepted the call. She joined herself to God's loving and saving will.

In freely surrendering herself to the will of the God who loved her, Mary followed the example of her son Jesus. The gospels recount decisive moments in the public life and ministry of Jesus when he reaffirmed his commitment to do the Father's will. The stories about Jesus' temptations and the agony in the garden capture the deep ways in which he surrendered himself to the Father's will. Jesus did not destroy his own will so that the Father's will could control him. He simply affirmed his relationship as the loving Son, who responded freely to the Father precisely because he was the loving Son.

Our own reaction and response to God's call may be mixed. We may not have a deep sense of being a loyal and loving son or daughter, as Jesus did. We may not be able to let go freely, to surrender without any conditions attached, as Mary did. Then how should we respond? First of all, it is important to realize that there are calls and invitations in our lives, but angels need not deliver them. They may come in the voice of another person, or in a special opportunity that comes our way, or in a longing rooted deep inside of us that will not go away. Whatever the form of delivery, the call is there. It may be a call to believe, perhaps in the face of grim circumstances. It may be a call to pray more or better or more deeply. It may be a call to serve in the Church or in the world in a way that will let God's love come alive. Whatever the shape of the call, there is no denying the presence of the call.

And our response? No doubt we may feel surprised and overwhelmed. But perhaps most of all, like Mary, we may feel afraid. We fear the loss of ourselves—that somehow we might become too involved. Reflecting on Mary's journey of faith may not completely remove our fears, but it certainly might lessen them. If we identify with Mary's experience of God's call, we know that all God wants is our loving freedom. We know that in surrendering ourselves we find ourselves in a better position than we ever were, because we find ourselves loved.

The Cost of
Accepting God's Call

In Matthew's gospel, Mary's journey of faith is joined to
Joseph's. The text reads: "Now the birth of Jesus the
Messiah took place in this way. When his mother Mary had
been engaged to Joseph, but before they lived together, she
was found to be with child from the Holy Spirit. Her husband
Joseph, being a righteous man and unwilling to expose her to
public disgrace, planned to dismiss her quietly. But just when
he had resolved to do this, an angel of the Lord appeared to
him in a dream and said, 'Joseph, son of David, do not be
afraid to take Mary as your wife, for the child conceived in her
is from the Holy Spirit. She will bear a son, and you are to
name him Jesus, for he will save his people from their sins.' All
this took place to fulfill what had been spoken by the Lord
through the prophet: 'Look, the virgin shall conceive and bear
a son, and they shall name him Emmanuel,' which means,
'God is with us.' When Joseph awoke from sleep, he did as the
angel of the Lord commanded him; he took her as his wife,
but had no marital relations with her until she had borne a
son; and he named him Jesus" (Matthew 1:18–25).

Joseph did not understand what had happened to Mary.
She, who was free and generous in responding to God's call,
was now very much misunderstood. She posed a riddle for
Joseph; he could not understand how she had conceived a
child. If we dwell on this scene and read between the lines,
another significant part of Mary's journey of faith surfaces.

Joseph's lack of understanding and his misunderstanding represent the price Mary had to pay for answering the Lord's call.

We know from experience that any call—to marriage, to religious life, to serve people as a doctor, nurse, or teacher—is not simply heard once and then answered once and for all. Any significant call involves a cost. If it is truly significant, it redirects a person's life, demands an investment of time and energy, and realigns relationships, sometimes in painful ways. In this sense, a call that is heard and answered needs to be reaffirmed when its consequences and its cost become evident.

When Mary experienced Joseph's misunderstanding, she experienced the price of her call. Her initial words of acceptance, "Let it be with me according to your word" (Luke 1:38), needed to be repeated. She had to draw her call into the whole fabric of her life and relationships, even into the intimate relationship with her husband-to-be. In other words, Mary needed to integrate her call into the whole of her life.

Eventually, a dream led Joseph to understand the sense and origin of Mary's pregnancy. This is not surprising. In dreams, a part of ourselves that moves beyond our ordinary way of thinking enables us to piece together what simple logic cannot explain. There are limits when it comes to understanding the ways of faith. We cannot always explain our reasons for doing things; sometimes we have reasons that are only known by the heart. It was something like that for Joseph. He came to an understanding of the situation through a dream, that special state in which mind and imagination and heart are blended.

Nevertheless, while Joseph was still trying to understand, Mary had to live with her decision and its consequences. She lived in a way that went against the expectations of her time, her culture, and her society. She had to live out her decision in a way that we might call countercultural. Only her gifted freedom, enabling her to keep saying yes, let her be faithful to her commitment in the face of serious misunderstanding.

We can identify with the cost Mary experienced in following her call. Anyone who follows a call pays some price. Perhaps there is a parallel between Mary's experience and the experience of many young people today. They may be aware of a call to live life different than their parents, perhaps more simply, perhaps in ways that would identify them with the poor or the oppressed. They are aware of the call, but their awareness comes through intuition; they feel that they cannot share their reasons with an older generation. Even though they have reasons, they cannot put them into words; but they are determined to remain faithful to their call, at times paying a heavy price in misunderstanding.

The "cost of discipleship" is a phrase made famous by the Lutheran theologian Dietrich Bonhoeffer, who authored a book by that title. His violent death at the hands of the Gestapo in 1945 gave eloquent witness to the price one must pay for following Jesus Christ. The cost of discipleship describes very well that part of Mary's journey of faith we have been considering. It also captures the meaning of the call that Jesus makes repeatedly in the gospels: "Leave all things and come and follow me."

According to Saint Luke, many people who heard that call "left everything and followed him" (Luke 5:11). That "everything" included what they could walk away from, such as family security, jobs, familiar surroundings, property, and possessions. It also included what they carried within themselves, such as their own sense of unworthiness, their feelings of insecurity, and the misunderstanding of family and friends.

To follow Jesus, to be his disciple, involves a cost. He made that abundantly clear as he called people. He even used the images of buying and selling to help people understand the cost of participating in the reign of God: "The kingdom of God is like treasure hidden in a field, which someone found and hid; then in his joy he goes and sells all that he has and buys that field. Again, the kingdom of heaven is like a merchant in search of fine pearls; on finding one pearl of great value, he went and sold all that he had and bought it" (Matthew 13:44–46).

Our first reaction to the gospels' teaching about the cost of discipleship may simply be to accept it as a warning. Yes, there is a price, and we should be ready to pay it. But there is more to it than that. The challenge moves beyond a warning and calls us to wrestle with the question of our freedom. We need to come to terms with the roots of our free decision in order to answer that call. Then, as the cost of the call and new challenges confront us, we can reaffirm and renew our free decision. With Mary, we can say again, as she had to say again, "Here am I, the servant of the Lord; let it be with me according to you word" (Luke 1:38).

Service:
Expression of the Call

In Mary's journey of faith, she not only heard and answered a call and experienced its cost, she also responded to that call through a life of service and sharing. Saint Luke captured that response in his description of Mary's visit to her cousin Elizabeth shortly after she received the angel's message. The text reads: "In those days Mary set out and went with haste to a Judean town in the hill country, where she entered the house of Zechariah and greeted Elizabeth. When Elizabeth heard Mary's greeting, the child leaped in her womb. And Elizabeth was filled with the Holy Spirit and exclaimed with a loud cry, 'Blessed are you among women, and blessed is the fruit of your womb. And why has this happened to me, that the mother of my Lord comes to me? For as soon as I heard the sound of your greeting, the child in my womb leaped for joy. And blessed is she who believed that there would be a fulfillment of what was spoken to her by the Lord.' And Mary said, 'My soul magnifies the Lord, and my spirit rejoices in God my Savior, for he has looked with favor on the lowliness of his servant. Surely, from now on all generations will call me blessed; for the Mighty One has done great things for me, and holy is his name . . .'" (Luke 1:39–49).

The passage tells us more than the story of a visit between two cousins, each expecting a baby. Mary's visit was a part of her response to God's call. The call, her acceptance of it, and her pregnancy had been drawn into her whole life in terms of their cost, especially the cost of misunderstanding. With the visit to Elizabeth, they entered the realm of service and sharing. Mary felt compelled to serve, to share what she was experiencing as a result of accepting God's demands on her life.

We know that no real love remains silent and unexpressed for very long. Our commitments and feelings need to find an outlet. We need engagement rings and birthday gifts. We need to do something for the people we love, even if it means some special and extra effort. Somehow, the word must get out about the way we feel. Somehow, actions have to follow on feelings and attachments. If Mary's journey to visit Elizabeth seems abrupt and unplanned to some people, it is because they have not understood how faith and love work. Mary had to share her story and some part of herself by serving.

The movement from an experience of faith to an expression of that faith in loving service and sharing is central to the preaching of Jesus. He tells us to be compassionate because we have experienced God's compassion in our own lives. He gives his disciples a new commandment to love one another because they have experienced his love for them. When faith and practice are separated, the result is a grotesque form of religion. The call of faith must be drawn into the various parts of our lives where it will find expression in service and in sharing what God has done. In a word, the teaching of Jesus and Mary's visit to Elizabeth present us with the challenge of a faith that is integrated into every part of our lives.

We share the challenge to draw our faith experience into the whole of our lives through service. The response to the challenge is one that we also share with the people of faith who have gone before us. It means searching for ways that are suitable and genuine, ways that will give expression to our faith in the God who has done great things for us. The search involves using our imagination and creativity. Just as people in love find unique ways of expressing their love for each other— personalized expressions of a love that cannot be duplicated—so too a part of our journey in faith involves looking for ways to express who we are and what we have become through our meeting with God.

Traveling with Joseph
to Bethlehem

L uke's gospel describes Mary's trip with Joseph to Bethlehem in two verses: "Joseph also went from the town of Nazareth in Galilee to Judea, to the city of David called Bethlehem, because he was descended from the house and family of David. He went to be registered with Mary, to whom he was engaged and who was expecting a child" (Luke 2:4–5). As in the scene of Mary's visit with Elizabeth, the details of Mary's trip with Joseph to Bethlehem are simple and straightforward. As we dwell on the story, however, we begin to see what traveling from Nazareth to Bethlehem meant for Mary's journey of faith.

The trip that Mary and Joseph made caused them to be uprooted. They had to leave familiar surroundings and the security that comes from being in touch with familiar faces and regular rhythms of life. Although leaving home is a physical act, experience tells us that no move from home is simply that; it involves an uprooting that reaches into the heart. Mary's journey of faith, as we have seen, had already brought a sense of uprootedness into her life. The message of the angel and her acceptance of the call were experiences of being uprooted, even without leaving Nazareth. The familiar and predictable pattern of life for a Nazareth girl of her time was significantly changed. She would no longer have the security she had come to know. Now the journey with Joseph to Bethlehem would add even more to her uprootedness.

People who leave their roots are very vulnerable people, subject to hurt. Only desperate circumstances or trust in a promised future enable people to be uprooted. Perhaps the story of Abraham came to Mary's mind as she set out from Nazareth. "Now the LORD said to Abram: 'Go from your country and your kindred and your father's house to the land that I will show you. . .' " (Genesis 12:1). The letter to the Hebrews speaks of Abraham's call and his response: "By faith Abraham obeyed when he was called to set out for a place that he was to receive as an inheritance; and he set out, not knowing where he was going" (Hebrews 11:8).

In faith, Mary and Joseph "set out." They were physically uprooted, but they found a rootedness in their faith, specifically in the One who was leading them. Mary had exchanged the security of her hometown life for a security based exclusively on trust in God's word. Elizabeth said: "Blessed is she who believed that there would be a fulfillment of what was spoken to her by the Lord" (Luke 1:45).

The journey with Joseph to Bethlehem also meant a waiting time. Much of the energy spent traveling has to do with simply "waiting to arrive." The waiting of Mary's journey coincided with the anticipation of her pregnancy. The time of carrying a child, like the time of traveling, goes by both slowly and quickly for the one waiting. There are little markers of time and space that indicate that progress is being made. But as long as one has not arrived, as long as the child is not born, the time is filled with waiting. In the waiting of the journey and the pregnancy, Mary kept vigil; she contemplated and watched. Just as her early life was marked by an openness to the word of God, so on the journey to Bethlehem, on her journey of faith, she watched and waited.

Mary's trip to Bethlehem was a shared journey; she went with Joseph. Of course, she traveled with Joseph on the road between Nazareth and Bethlehem, but she also traveled with him in a journey of faith. Although it did not happen easily, although there was an initial misunderstanding, Mary's journey of faith as she heard the call of God and accepted it was a journey made with a companion. The two of them came together in the name of Jesus, and journeying together anticipated the community of disciples to be gathered in his name, the community of faith to which we belong.

We can map out our own lives as journeys that hold experiences similar to those of Mary and Joseph. Even if we do not move physically from one locale to another, our lives are in motion. For a number of years, the study of child psychology has given us an appreciation of the developments that take place in childhood. Only recently has psychology alerted us to adult development. We grow and change even after we reach that magical age of twenty-one. Young adults struggle to achieve a place in this world, in their work, in their social life, and in their interpersonal relations. People entering midlife undergo the "midlife crisis." People in their later years apply themselves to the delicate task of sorting through life in order to make sense out of the whole of it. Through the journey of adult development, times and seasons of uprootedness occur. Leaving one's family, changing jobs, having children, leaving a younger generation to join an older one, the death of one's parents, the limits of illness—all these mark the times of uprootedness.

A life journey involves a waiting and watching time. Sometimes we can only catch the motion of our lives when we are at rest, when we are at times of life review. Then we take a look at ourselves and at our experiences and reach the insight that we are on the way or, better, on a way that we can accept or change or to which we can resign ourselves.

The setbacks and advances of a life journey depend in great measure on one's companions along the way. Sometimes, special people accompany us—friends, spouses, or mentors—people who provide us with models of how life can be lived or things can be accomplished. Sometimes less tangible, but no less real, companions walk with us. They may be dreams and visions, hopes and plans, or a presence loving and greater than ourselves. However we consider the journey, the companions are essential to complete it.

The believer's life is a life that shares the human drama, with its times of uprootedness, vigilant watchfulness, and companionship. The believer's journey also follows the example of Jesus. According to Luke's gospel, "When the days drew near for him to be taken up, he set his face to go to Jerusalem . . ." (Luke 9:51). Jesus also experienced times of uprootedness, culminating in Jerusalem and the cross. He was vigilant and watchful, regularly gathering every aspect of his life and ministry and surrendering it into the hands of his Father. He traveled in the companionship of his disciples, but also in the presence of the Holy Spirit and his Father. His dream and vision of the reign of God sparked his teaching, his healing, and his plans for his followers. Although we can identify our journey with the journey of Mary and Joseph, we acknowledge that it finds its source of power in Jesus.

The Birth of Jesus

The gospel of Luke describes the birth of Jesus very simply: "And she gave birth to her firstborn son and wrapped him in bands of cloth, and laid him in a manger. . ." (Luke 2:7). This brief description does not quite do justice to what every mother knows, however. Giving birth to a child and becoming a mother reshapes the life of a woman. In a real sense, she herself is reborn when she gives birth to her baby. Mary's experience was like that of every other mother.

The infant Jesus, like all newborns, made infinite claims and demands on his parents. Apart from modern conveniences, such as disposable diapers, taking care of babies—with their endless claims and demands—has hardly changed over thousands of years. The story then is the story now, of middle-of-the-night feedings, changing clothes, rocking to sleep, adjusting the blankets. The infant Jesus not only made endless claims and demands; he also signaled infinite promise and unlimited possibilities. Perhaps at no other time of life is so much hope thrown in our direction as when we are first born. We are little bundles of seemingly pure potential.

Mary held the newborn Jesus; she held the demands and the claims, the promise and the possibilities. Mary, the woman journeying in faith, held the child she had conceived in faith. The demands and claims of faith had become clear in her call, and she answered yes in freedom and love. The promise of faith took root in her call. She proclaimed the goodness of God and God's faithfulness to the promises made to Abraham and his descendants forever. Now it all came together. The demands and claims and promise and possibility were as specific as the child she held. Her journey of faith did not bring her to dream the impossible dream or to follow some vague and perhaps abstract ideal. Her journey led her to hold the flesh of the Word made flesh, who came to dwell among us. In her child's birth, she was reborn; her faith was renewed.

The birth of Jesus was not a private event. As the gospels describe it, the birth of Jesus involved people other than Jesus, Mary, and Joseph. These people ranged from the poor and devout to the highly educated to the evil and scheming. The birth of Jesus occurred in a crosscut of humanity that represented the best and worst of who we can be. Shepherds, poor people who could hear angels, came to visit the newborn Jesus. Magi, wise men of the East who had been searching for signs, came and found the child with his mother. "They knelt down and paid him homage. Then, opening their treasure chests, they offered him gifts of gold, frankincense, and myrrh" (Matthew 2:11b–12). There was also King Herod who had heard the question of the wise men, "Where is the child who has been born king of the Jews?" (Matthew 2:2). He felt a threat to his own kingship and began to search for the child to destroy him.

The visits of the shepherds and the Magi, as well as the threats of King Herod, bring us to a special intersection of Mary's faith journey. Her personal, private, and domestic life crosses over into public, historical, and even political life. In faith she gave birth to her child, but this was not merely an event enclosed in her personal, private, and domestic world. The one to whom she gave birth was destined to be for the poor waiting people of Israel, represented by the shepherds. He was also meant to be a light for all the nations, the Gentile world as well as the people of Israel. He represented the reign of God coming into this world, and therefore he stands as a challenge to all political power that looks upon itself as a power unto itself.

In the birth of Jesus, as previously mentioned, Mary was reborn. Her journey of faith took new shape as she held the child she had conceived in faith. She found her life changed, her faith and what flowed from it drawn into the public, historical, and political arenas of life. We find a resonance and a challenge in Mary's experience. We are reborn many times into new life and renewed faith.

The more striking examples of being reborn belong to people who have weathered serious illnesses. After they find themselves healed, they often remark that they feel they have been given another chance, a new lease on life. They are the same, yet different. They see autumn leaves and children playing in the park, sunsets and starlight with new eyes, as if seeing these things for the first time. They value their relationships with friends, spouse, and family in a new way, no longer presuming the presence and love of people as they might have previously. They discover a new patience in situations that once would have caused them to bristle. They size up little things as little things and recognize what is truly big and important. If they stop to think about it, they find themselves with a renewed sense of gratitude and responsibility. Gratitude for being healed and restored spills over into other areas of life. At the same time, their new lease on life pulls them into a new sense that they are responsible, that they must take life seriously.

Although recovering from a serious illness is a dramatic way to experience a rebirth, there is a more subtle, more powerful way in which this happens. As we come to terms with the loving movement of God in our lives, we also experience being reborn; we receive a new lease on life. We begin to see things differently. Both positive and negative life situations, such as succeeding in business or stumbling in our own weakness, take on a different meaning. We not only look at life, we begin to see it. We move beyond appearances into the substance of things, and take in the big picture of life.

Relationships with other people hold new value because being in touch with God makes us aware that love endures. We feel regular stirrings of gratitude because we know that so little of what we see, hear, touch, and are is of our own making. It is given. A growing sense of responsibility follows on the gratitude we feel. Faith links us in a fundamental way with God and with one another. Faith thus moves us out of a simply personal world into sharing the concerns and struggles of others.

At particular moments of reflection or crisis or celebration, we hold the consequences of our faith in our hands, just as Mary held the newborn child in hers. We face, as she did, the very real demands and claims and promise and possibilities of that faith. Faith takes flesh in the concrete circumstances of life. When that happens, we are being reborn. Our lives are reshaped.

In the Temple

In the second chapter of Luke's gospel, we find two stories about Jesus, Mary, and Joseph that took place in the temple of Jerusalem. The events described are traditionally called the presentation in the temple and the finding in the temple. Although they center on Jesus, the stories also help us understand Mary's journey of faith. In both events, she was joined to her son; in both instances, she was called upon to exercise her faith.

The first story is about the presentation, which occurred shortly after the birth of Jesus. "When the time came for their purification according to the law of Moses, they brought him up to Jerusalem to present him to the Lord (as it is written in the law of the Lord, 'Every firstborn male shall be designated as holy to the Lord'), and they offered a sacrifice according to what is stated in the law of the Lord, 'a pair of turtledoves or two young pigeons'" (Luke 2:22–24).

Luke underscores the sense of duty that led Mary and Joseph to present Jesus in the temple. They followed the law of Moses and acted in accord with its prescriptions. Mary and Joseph, after all, shared the covenant faith of Israel. They followed the law with deep conviction—it was not merely an impersonal prescription that had to be followed. It embodied and expressed God's covenant love for Israel: "You shall be my people, and I will be your God" (Ezekiel 36:28b).

To follow the law, then, and to act in accord with it meant being faithful to God's love. To bring the newborn Jesus to the temple, to present him, and to offer sacrifice "according to what is stated in the law of the Lord" were acts of dutiful love, not the fulfillment of legalistic requirements.

While they were in the temple, Simeon, an old man who was waiting for the fulfillment of God's promises to Israel, was moved by the Holy Spirit to recognize the presence of the Messiah in the newborn Jesus. After praising God, he addressed these mysterious words to Mary: "This child is destined for the falling and the rising of many in Israel, and to be a sign that will be opposed so that the inner thoughts of many will be revealed—and a sword will pierce your own soul too" (Luke 2:34b–35).

Then, Anna, an old and holy woman known as a prophetess, approached the family. "At that moment she came, and began to praise God and to speak about the child to all who were looking for the redemption of Jerusalem" (Luke 2:38). The family left Jerusalem to return to Nazareth after fulfilling what the law of Moses required. As they returned, there must have been a sense of bewilderment about the meaning of their meeting with Simeon and Anna.

The second story also took place in the temple of Jerusalem, when Jesus was twelve. Once again, Mary and Joseph as devout children of Israel went to Jerusalem to celebrate the Passover, recalling how God had led the people of Israel out of the slavery of Egypt. After the celebration had ended, they prepared to return to Nazareth. Saint Luke wrote: "When the festival was ended and they started to return, the boy Jesus stayed behind in Jerusalem, but his parents did not know it. Assuming that he was in the group of travelers, they went a day's journey. Then they started to look for him among their relatives and friends. When they did not find him, they returned to Jerusalem to search for him. After three days they found him in the temple, sitting among the teachers, listening to them and asking them questions. And all who heard him were amazed at his understanding and his answers. When his parents saw him they were astonished; and his mother said to him, 'Child why have you treated us like this? Look, your father and I have been searching for you in great anxiety.' He said to them, 'Why were you searching for me? Did you not know that I must be in my Father's house?' But they did not understand what he said to them" (Luke 2:43–50). Luke clearly lets us know about the puzzlement of Mary; she and Joseph could not understand what had happened, or even the words of Jesus.

Both stories are steeped in a sense of bewilderment. Simeon and Anna spoke of the child, his destiny and his greatness, in terms that left his parents wondering. They were bewildered again when they found twelve-year-old Jesus in the temple. On both occasions, Mary's journey of faith led her to meet the claims of God. They were claims, however, that reached beyond what she might have expected. She heard things about the direction and future life of Jesus that moved well beyond the expectations a family has for a child. The mission of Jesus and his destiny were already becoming evident, but in ways that Mary could not understand.

We can identify with Mary's experience in the temple. The experience is that of not knowing, of pieces not coming together, of wondering how the claims of God fit into the total picture of life. Although she did not understand, she did two things: she trusted and she contemplated. Her silence after the words of Simeon and Anna and after the words of Jesus spoken in the temple is the language of her acceptance, even though she did not understand. She also contemplated, pondering the experiences and the words. According to Saint Luke, after the finding in the temple, "he went down with them and came to Nazareth, and was obedient to them. His mother treasured all these things in her heart" (Luke 2:51). She contemplated in trust. In other words, she allowed herself to dwell on the words and experiences in Jerusalem with the hope of gaining a wider sense of the claims of God on her son and on her own life.

In addition to her contemplation in trust, we can detect another side of Mary's faith. She did not falter because she was puzzled and did not understand. That she could live with words and experiences without understanding them means that somehow she had identified them as parts of a larger whole. Bewilderment would not dominate her life; they could not be read as setbacks and insurmountable obstacles to her future or her son's future. We know from our own experience how a part of living, such as illness, accident, loss, or success, can invade one's life and become the whole of it. The part substitutes for the whole. But Mary was not stopped by the partial character of the moment; she put her trust in a future fullness.

We might consider some of our own expectations of a life of faith. Among these expectations we should certainly hope for a greater clarity about the sense and the direction of our lives. Perhaps the most obvious instance of the tension between our expectations and the reality of the journey of faith occurs when we must face an important loss. The loss may be the death of someone close to us. Almost instinctively we ask, "Why did God do this? Why did God allow this to happen? What does it mean?"

When we raise these questions, we are painfully aware of our own bewilderment. We are puzzled by the claims of God at that moment. Perhaps the questions, formulated when the feeling of loss is intense, mean that we have taken the present moment to represent the whole of life. The challenge to our own journey of faith offered by Mary's journey is to imitate her response. In the face of confusion, we are called to contemplate in trust. We are called to allow ourselves to dwell on the words and experiences of our lives with the hope of gaining a wider sense of the claims of God on it.

At Nazareth

L uke concludes the story of the finding in the temple with two verses we have already seen: "Then he went down with them and came to Nazareth, and was obedient to them. His mother treasured all these things in her heart. And Jesus increased in wisdom and in years, and in divine and human favor" (Luke 2:51–52). About eighteen years of Mary's life are contained in this passage. So if we want to continue tracing her journey of faith, it is important to understand the life of Mary at Nazareth.

To imagine life at Nazareth in biblical times means that we must put aside preconceived images; we need to strip away the antiseptic pictures of some popular religious art. Today's parallels to Nazareth will not be found in home decor magazines or in beautiful suburban homes or on television. To speak of Nazareth is to speak of poor people, people who worked hard and did not have much to show for their labor. The people of Nazareth lived in a basic way.

Although the level of material possessions, comforts, or consumption that we are accustomed to was unknown, there was a richness of humanity in the style of life. The people of Nazareth shared a basic and humanly rich rhythm of life. It included eating, working, resting, playing, knowing each other, being known, transmitting values, telling stories. When we can picture Nazareth as materially poor and humanly rich, we begin to understand the real Nazareth of the Bible. This was the environment in which

Jesus grew up, and in which Mary continued her journey of faith.

Although poverty obviously implies a lack of material wealth, we would be mistaken to limit it exclusively to material things. There is another concept of poverty that is religious, and not merely social and economic. In the Old Testament, the "poor of Israel," the *anawim*, refers to those who are in need of God and are open to his will. Their poverty is linked mainly with the possibilities of faith, not with destitution. Their lives reflect the covenant faith of Israel. They sense their dependence on God. They deeply feel a need for God's saving power in their own relatively powerless lives. The *anawim* remember God and know their dependence. Israel recalled the great acts of God when the people of Israel were especially mindful of God and their dependence on him. God led a poor enslaved people out of Egypt. God brought back a poor exiled people to their land. God called a poor young girl of Nazareth to be the mother of the Messiah.

The poverty of Nazareth made Mary especially susceptible to the movement of God in her life. This poverty was the background for the preaching of Jesus. Especially in Luke's gospel, we find that Jesus clearly and pointedly proclaimed the good news to the poor, those genuinely open to receive his word. He said, "Blessed are you who are poor, for yours is the kingdom of God" (Luke 6:20b). The reign of God belongs to those who are not owned by anything else. In the face of material possessions, Jesus poses the sharp question of our root identity. What is at the heart of our lives—what we *have* or who we *are*? "What does it profit them if they gain the whole world, but lose or forfeit themselves?" (Luke 9:25).

The faith of Israel, the words of Jesus, and the life of Mary at Nazareth have left deep marks on the lives of believers over the course of two thousand years. The words and examples found in the Bible have a power because they have a rightness about them. Saint Ignatius of Loyola, the founder of the Society of Jesus (the Jesuits), connected his conversion from being a worldly soldier to a committed believer with hearing the penetrating question of Jesus "What does it profit them if they gain the whole world . . . ?" Francis of Assisi, the founder of the Franciscans, gave up his family fortune to devote himself to preaching, prayer, and the service of the poor.

The social teaching of the Church has often stressed and spoken of the privileged position of the poor in the Old Testament and the gospels. The Church invites us to a preferential love of the poor. Whatever the form of expression, whatever the means employed, the witness of countless believers who have gone before us also invites and urges us to come to terms with our own poverty. In this, we join our journey of faith with Mary.

To understand Mary's faith development at Nazareth, we can look to a parable of Jesus about the reign of God. The story that Jesus used was no doubt drawn from his own experience at home. "He told them another parable: 'The kingdom of heaven is like yeast that a woman took and mixed in with three measures of flour until all of it was leavened' " (Matthew 13:33). Whenever I read this parable, I connect it with experiences of my childhood. I remember watching my grandmother make bread. She would take the flour, salt, water, oil, and yeast, and mix them together. After kneading the dough, she set it aside. Later I would see her come back and uncover the dough; it was always a surprise to see how the dough had risen. Quietly and gradually, the yeast leavened the dough, and it rose. The yeast seemed to contain a very steady and seemingly indomitable power within itself.

The action of the yeast, the coming of the reign of God, and Mary's faith development at Nazareth can all be described as quiet and gradual, but powerfully steady in their movement. For Mary, this movement involved every area of her experience at Nazareth. She "treasured all these things in her heart," according to Luke; she kept in her heart and pondered deep within her the experiences of her call, the birth of her son, and the events surrounding his early life.

Keeping things in her heart, however, does not mean a kind of sentimental and nostalgic attachment to events of the past. Mary kept the events alive in her heart in order to ponder their meaning and understand where they would lead her and her son. More important, Mary was deeply present to her son. For Mary, to see him and watch him meant to see and watch the promise of God in her life and in the life of her people. As a wife and mother, she also had the ordinary interests of her family and village to tend to. Whatever was involved in caring for people, sustaining and supporting them, was a part of Mary's experience at Nazareth. She developed quietly and gradually, but with the steady and indomitable power of faith.

All this may not seem to be much to us. Perhaps our assessment is distorted by the desire to see growth only in dramatic accomplishments. The way of Nazareth was a little way, an ordinary way. The patterns of development at Nazareth, just as surely as the poverty of Nazareth, call us to reconsider the way we think about our own journey of faith. Its development takes place in surprising ways, ways that are quiet and gradual and yet very powerful.

Apart from any specific religious concerns, a number of voices today are calling for the "simple" life. Perhaps contained in this appeal is a hidden insight about the way of Nazareth—simple, hidden, ordinary.

The Beginning
of Jesus' Ministry

I n the gospels, reference is made to Mary two times at the
beginning of Jesus' public ministry. The first time is at the
wedding in Cana. The passage reads: "On the third day there
was a wedding in Cana of Galilee, and the mother of Jesus
was there. Jesus and his disciples had also been invited to the
wedding. When the wine gave out, the mother of Jesus said
to him, 'They have no wine.' And Jesus said to her, 'Woman,
what concern is that to you and to me? My hour has not yet
come.' His mother said to the servants, 'Do whatever he tells
you.' Now standing there were six stone water jars for the
Jewish rites of purification, each holding twenty or thirty
gallons. Jesus said to them, 'Fill the jars with water.' And they
filled them up to the brim. He said to them, 'Now draw some
out, and take it to the chief steward.' So they took it. When
the steward tasted the water that had become wine, and did
not know where it came from (though the servants who had
drawn the water knew), the steward called the bridegroom
and said to him, 'Everyone serves the good wine first, and
then the inferior wine after the guests have become drunk.
But you have kept the good wine until now.' Jesus did this, the
first of his signs, in Cana of Galilee, and revealed his glory; and
his disciples believed in him" (John 2:1–11).

Viewed as a whole, the story of Cana belongs primarily to
the story of Jesus. Cana is where he performed his first sign,
where he revealed his glory. Nevertheless, Mary plays an
important part; her presence is felt from the very first

sentence. Since we are considering Mary's journey of faith, we will look at the story from her point of view.

The first and most obvious detail of the story is Mary's presence. She was with Jesus. Her presence was a natural part of her faith journey. As a pregnant young woman, she carried him; at Nazareth, she mothered him; and as Jesus began his ministry at Cana, she accompanied him. Her words, "They have no wine," confirm what we have known all along: that she was a serving and loving person, sensitive to others and their needs. Implied in her observation was a request directed to Jesus that led to an unusual exchange of words between them. He seemed to resist her request because his hour had not yet come. Her reaction was to place complete trust in her son. She said to the waiters, "Do whatever he tells you." And he provided more wine.

Mary joined the mission and ministry of Jesus. In fact, according to John's gospel, her presence framed the entire public ministry of Jesus. She was with him at Cana in the beginning of his ministry; she stood at the foot of the cross at its end. In being with him, Mary showed very clearly what it means to be a follower of Jesus; her life was linked with his mission. At the same time, she must have wondered at his reply to her. She did not understand the meaning and scope of his mission. That was nothing new, of course. Recall her confusion in the temple at the presentation and finding of Jesus. Mary's journey of faith led her not only to be with Jesus but also to enter more deeply into the meaning of his mission.

A similar challenge appears in Mark's gospel, again near the beginning of Jesus' ministry. The passage from Mark reads: "Then his mother and his brothers came; and standing outside, they sent to him and called him. A crowd was sitting around him; and they said to him, 'Your mother and your brothers and sisters are outside, asking for you.' And he replied, 'Who are my mother and my brothers?' And looking at those who sat around him, he said, 'Here are my mother and my brothers! Whoever does the will of God is my brother and sister and mother'" (Mark 3:31–34).

The words of Jesus contain a strong and startling message, one that is central to his teaching: a relationship is established with him by doing the will of God, and the bonds of that relationship are family bonds. Jesus affirms the existence of a new family of God whose bonds are even stronger than those of blood, since it is brought about by doing the will of God. Family relationships based merely on blood ties are weak in comparison.

Reflecting on the passage from Mark's gospel can give us a new insight into Mary's journey of faith. She had the painful but unavoidable experience of every parent. The day arrives when a child is no longer a child, but an adult. The mother must let go so that the child can be an independent adult.

It may be easy in principle to talk about "letting go," but in reality it can be very painful. The mother's desire and commitment from the moment of birth is to nurture and support her child, using all that she has and is. As the child becomes an adult, that commitment to nurture must be changed into a new type of support. She has to trust the child as he or she moves beyond the walls of the family home. Like all mothers, Mary had to adjust her thinking to this fact of life.

Although she would still be with him, it would be in a new way.

But there was something unique about Mary's letting go. The demands being made upon her were even greater than those made on other mothers because the demands were rooted in special claims of God. Mary had already met the claims of God at the announcement of the birth of Jesus and then again in the temple. Now, the claims of God would take specific shape in the acceptance of her son's message and preaching. A new family of God was coming about, one made up of those joined to her son not by the ties of blood but by doing the will of God.

When Mary heard her son's words, "Whoever does the will of God is my brother and sister and mother" (Mark 3:34), she must have heard an echo of her own words spoken at the annunciation, "Here am I, the servant of the Lord; let it be with me according to your word" (Luke 1:38). She could recognize in herself the very commitment that Jesus asked of his followers, those who would be brother or sister or mother to him—the commitment to do the will of God. This placed Mary at the center of the new family of God. Her journey of faith was a journey home. She was part of a family with bonds stronger than blood. She could see herself in a new way as the mother of Jesus.

If we want to connect our journey of faith with the moment of Mary's journey when Jesus spoke of the new family of God, we should ask ourselves, "Who belongs to me? To whom do I belong?" We simply cannot survive as detached, free-floating agents in this world. We need to belong. We need to feel that we are a part of the lives of other people, and that others are a part of our lives. In a word, we need to feel at home. The opposite is what philosophers and sociologists call the feeling of alienation, the feeling of not-at-homeness. So the question is not whether we will belong to others or others to us; the question is how and to whom.

As we face these questions, we hear the call of Jesus to follow him, to belong to him and through him to one another in the new family of God. Yet when we hear the demands of following him and belonging to him, we may reel back because the words seem to be harsh, even unbearable. We hear echoes of the sharp words in Mark's gospel that seem to set Jesus apart from his natural family: "Whoever does the will of God is my brother and sister and mother" (Mark 3:35). The words seem to be pointed even more in our direction when we hear the words of Jesus to would-be followers: "As they were going along the road, someone said to him, 'I will follow you wherever you go.' And Jesus said to him, 'Foxes have holes, and birds of the air have nests; but the Son of Man has nowhere to lay his head.' To another he said, 'Follow me.' But he said, 'Lord, first let me go and bury my father.' But Jesus said to him, 'Let the dead bury their own dead; but as for you, go and proclaim the kingdom of God.' Another said, 'I will follow you, Lord; but let me first say farewell to those at my home.' Jesus said to him, 'No one who puts a hand to the plow and looks back is fit for the kingdom of God' " (Luke 9:57–62).

The demands of discipleship, of belonging to Jesus, seem to place inhuman and impossible burdens on us; they uproot us from family and home. Those who listened to Jesus, for example, must have been shocked to hear him seemingly dismiss the obligation to bury one's parents. The language is uncompromisingly strong.

If we are faced with a choice between family or Jesus, perhaps we should turn for guidance to Mary's experience in her journey of faith. She too faced difficult choices. From her experience, we can begin to piece together the sense and meaning of the call of Jesus. The words about following the Son of Man who has no place to lay his head, or about letting the dead bury their dead, or about not even saying farewell to the people at home, call to mind the way Mary had to let go of her son. She was required not only to let go of Jesus so that he could fulfill his adult mission, she was also required to let go of the old ways. Jesus proclaims a new life in the coming of the reign of God. Only those who let go of the old can accept and live in a new way.

So understood, the appeal of Jesus to let go is still valid for us today. It means breaking with our expectations of how life ought to be, breaking with whatever would hold us back from God's new thing. Letting go invades the deepest parts of our lives, even family relationships.

The other side of Mary's experience can also guide us on our journey of faith. She not only let go, she also found herself bound far more closely than by ties of blood. If the demands of Jesus seem harsh, inhuman, and impossible, this may be because we have separated the demands from the promise. We hear the cost without understanding the gain. As we let go, we do not find ourselves out in the cold; on the contrary, we find ourselves at home with a family. The difference is that the home is now our home more than ever. The family is closer than one may have thought possible. Now, it is not blood relationships that hold home and family together; it is our relationship with God, the loving source and destiny of our lives, that does so.

Every follower of Jesus, Mary included, faces the critical questions "Who belongs to me?" and "To whom do I belong?" Their journey of faith brings them to this conclusion: All relationships need to be reshaped in light of the new relationship with God in Jesus. Concretely, this means that people must trustingly let go to refind themselves in the new family of God.

Observing the
Ministry of Jesus

O nce the public ministry of Jesus begins, the New Testament is silent about Mary. Reference is made to her once again in John's gospel in the scene at the foot of the cross; she is also mentioned in the opening chapter of the Acts of the Apostles. Apart from Cana and the scene in Mark's gospel (with its parallels in Matthew and Luke) already referred to, Mary's presence during the public ministry of Jesus was a quiet and hidden presence. Whether or not she traveled with him, she was with him or present to him in some way during that time. Her son continued to be the object of her attention and concern; she contemplated what he did and said. We can follow the details of this part of her faith journey by observing the ministry of her son.

A good place to begin is with a speech made by Peter some time after the death and resurrection of Jesus. The speech, found in the Acts of the Apostles, contains a brief summary of the public ministry of Jesus. Peter said: "You know the message [God] sent to the people of Israel, preaching peace by Jesus Christ—he is Lord of all. That message spread throughout Judea, beginning in Galilee after the baptism that John announced: how God anointed Jesus of Nazareth with the Holy Spirit and with power; how he went about doing good and healing all who were oppressed by the devil, for God was with him. We are witnesses to all that he did both in Judea and in Jerusalem" (Acts 10:36–39).

Peter went on to describe the death and resurrection of Jesus, events we will consider in later sections. For now, it is important to see what Jesus did during his public ministry. He appeared as one filled with the Spirit of God, endowed with power. People could see the presence of God in the many forms that his ministry took.

Peter's words in the Acts of the Apostles run parallel to a passage found in Luke's gospel that describes an occasion at the beginning of the public ministry of Jesus when he preached in his hometown of Nazareth. The passage reads: "When he came to Nazareth, where he had been brought up, he went to the synagogue on the sabbath day, as was his custom. He stood up to read, and the scroll of the prophet Isaiah was given to him. He unrolled the scroll and found the place where it was written: 'The spirit of the Lord is upon me, because he has anointed me to bring good news to the poor. He has sent me to proclaim release to the captives and recovery of sight to the blind, to let the oppressed go free, to proclaim the year of the Lord's favor.' And he rolled up the scroll, gave it back to the attendant, and sat down. The eyes of all in the synagogue were fixed on him. Then he began to say to them, 'Today this scripture has been fulfilled in your hearing'" (Luke 4:16–21).

As we read this passage, we begin to get a picture of the scope of Jesus' mission and public ministry. One detail seems to be essential: He was sent to bring glad tidings. But what precisely are the glad tidings he brings? What exactly is the good news he proclaims? To answer these questions, we can turn to the beginning of Mark's gospel where the core of the preaching of Jesus is described: "Now after John was arrested, Jesus came to Galilee, proclaiming the good news of God, and saying, 'The time is fulfilled, and the kingdom of God has come near; repent, and believe in the good news' " (Mark 1:14–15).

The good news is that the reign of God is upon us; God's reign is taking hold of us at this very moment. It means that God is taking hold of our lives, that all things are coming together as they should. The reign of God means that we belong to God entirely and that God belongs to us entirely. We belong to the kingdom described in the Mass of Christ the King as "an eternal and universal kingdom: a kingdom of truth and life, a kingdom of holiness and grace, a kingdom of justice, love, and peace."

Mary, the journeying woman of faith open to the possibilities offered by God, heard her son proclaim the good news of the reign of God. Mary not only heard the proclamation of the good news, but—like Peter, who was a witness "to all that he did both in Judea and in Jerusalem"—she understood that Jesus' words and deeds show the reign of God has already broken into our lives.

A new way of understanding, which is part of the reign of God, emerges in the teachings of Jesus. When he teaches through parables, stories drawn from daily life, Jesus turns our way of thinking around. If we think that being repentant means being sad, we need to change our way of thinking. Repentance is as joyful as a shepherd finding a lost sheep, or a woman recovering money lost in her house. If we think that mercy is only for our receiving and not for our giving, we should think about the forgiven servant who went out and put pressure on a fellow servant who owed him a small amount. If we think that God plays favorites, look at the sun and the rain and how they shine and fall on everyone. The reign of

God means new life and, therefore, a new, fresh way of thinking.

The reign of God also means a new way of living, a new faithfulness that does not cut corners or hedge bets. When Jesus argued with the scribes and the Pharisees, the professional religious people of his day, he called them to a new faithfulness. It is not enough, he said, to measure your faithfulness to God simply by external observances. What counts is what comes from the heart.

The reign of God means full of life, and this means health and wholeness. Jesus helped a woman stand straight who had been stooped for years. When lepers wanted relief from their physically and socially painful disease, he cured them. As he healed the physical ailments of people, Jesus proclaimed the healing power that was taking hold of them in the reign of God.

There is no room in God's reign for relationships with him that are broken. This is why Jesus forgave the sins of people, even if they did not ask him. He knew and he proclaimed that God's mercy has no limits. It reaches out to everyone—and not just once, but over and over again. The reign of God means that peace with God and with one another is taking hold of our lives.

The reign of God also means, as we have seen, gathering people into the new family of God. Jesus proclaimed this aspect of the reign of God as he gathered followers around him. He fed them as a sign of the abundance that marks the reign of God. He formed them through his message. Then he empowered them and sent them out to share the good news.

The reign of God is a network of relationships held together in God's hands.

In her journey of faith, Mary observed her son proclaiming the reign of God in his teaching, in calling people to faithfulness, in healing, in forgiving sin, in gathering the family of God. In faith, she came to recognize along with his other followers that "God was with him." She also probably realized that the reign of God, God's dream for the human family, was not only being proclaimed by her son in the different areas of his public ministry, but that he himself was the breaking in of the reign of God. In other words, through observing him and being with him, Mary came to know the signs of the reign of God: understanding, faithfulness, wholeness, compassion, gathering, justice, and peace. With that she would understand that Jesus is the sign and the living presence of the reign of God among us. Her journey of faith moved closely with the ministry of Jesus.

Our own journey of faith must somehow follow the example of Mary. We need to hear the basic good news that the reign of God is at hand. We need to have a change of heart and to believe in the good news. We need to follow the arrival of the reign of God in the ministry of Jesus and to recognize how the reign of God affects us. We need to learn to "read the signs of the time," as Blessed John XXIII said, in order to be able to detect the very real and concrete ways that the reign of God is already upon us. Perhaps even more challenging, we need to plot out the reign of God in our own lives and in the world around us. Then we can join with Mary and all the followers of Jesus in praying as he taught us: Thy kingdom come.

The Suffering and Death of Jesus

E ventually, the preaching and good works of Jesus led him into a number of conflicts. Some of the established religious leaders saw Jesus as a threat to the delicate balance of peace with the occupying Roman armies. Others considered his claim to forgive sins as blasphemy, an insult hurled against God. Some of his own followers walked away from him in disbelief. One of Jesus' specially chosen disciples, Judas Iscariot, betrayed him and handed him over to the authorities. The conflicts stirred up in various quarters by the preaching and ministry of Jesus intensified and eventually led to his execution on the cross. He suffered the death of a common criminal in the Roman style—by crucifixion.

The death of Jesus has been examined from many different viewpoints. Some have seen it as a political action. Others have considered it the result of betrayal by a friend. Believers have understood it as reparation for the sins of humankind, as being for our salvation. The words of Jesus in John's Gospel explain it this way: "For God so loved the world that he gave his only Son, so that everyone who believes in him may not perish but may have eternal life" (John 3:16). The death of Jesus was a death *for us*; it represented an unmistakable sign of love.

At the hour of his death, Mary was with Jesus at the cross. John's gospel recounts the scene: "Standing near the cross of Jesus were his mother, and his mother's sister, Mary the wife of Clopas, and Mary Magdalene. When Jesus saw his mother and the disciple whom he loved standing beside her, he said to his mother, 'Woman, here is your son.' Then he said to the disciple, 'Here is your mother.' And from that hour the disciple took her into his own home" (John 19:25–27). In her journey of faith, Mary followed her son as his first and closest disciple. It was fitting that at the end of his earthly life Jesus would give his mother to the beloved disciple, one who represented all who follow Jesus. She belongs to the community of all who follow Jesus; she is the mother of all his disciples.

Perhaps we can enter the scene of the crucifixion and try to realize what that moment meant to Mary in her journey of faith. As Mary was standing before the cross, she stood before what appeared to be the end of a dream, the collapse of a great hope. Her cousin Elizabeth had said, "Blessed is she who believed that there would be a fulfillment of what was spoken to her by the Lord" (Luke 1:45). In her faith, Mary was a woman of promise, a woman who lived from what God offered her. Her son Jesus was a child of her faith, a child of promise. As she journeyed with him, listening to the things people said about him and piecing together things from her own experience of God's call, her hope intensified. In what he did and said, Jesus appeared as the presence of the reign of God taking hold of our world. Now she was standing before the cross. The dream seemed ended.

Suffering touches all of our lives, but not all suffering is the same. One type of suffering results from the collapse of our possibilities. It occurs when all our options seem to be closed down. It is connected with a sense of the dead-endness of what could have been. This is the suffering people endure when they themselves or those close to them are diagnosed as having a terminal illness. This is the suffering of a family in which one of the members suffers from alcoholism. This is the suffering seen at a wake, after the death of a young person in an accident. Whether it is a terminal illness or alcoholism or a tragic accident, all these experiences cut off possibilities, narrow our choices, and seem to lead us nowhere. The suffering is especially intense in these experiences because we keep thinking about what could have been or what ought to have been.

If we join Mary at the cross, we meet this kind of suffering. It is utterly intense because it is connected with what could have been and what ought to have been. Mary's pain was not lessened because of her faith, nor will it be for us—faith is not a painkiller. Rather, because of her faith, Mary responded with trust. Her trust was not grounded in the details of the situation, which seemed to offer no hope, but on God's faithfulness. "He has helped his servant Israel, in remembrance of his mercy; according to the promise he made to our ancestors, to Abraham and to his descendants forever" (Luke 1:54–55).

Mary's belief in God's faithfulness allowed her to hope that this suffering was ultimately a suffering of passage, that this suffering would lead beyond itself and not to a dead end. This is the teaching of Jesus and the meaning of the cross. "Very truly, I tell you, unless a grain of wheat falls into the earth and dies, it remains just a single grain; but if it dies, it bears much fruit" (John 12:24). This, too, is the prayer of the Church in the Mass for the dead: "Lord, for your faithful people life is changed, not ended." This was Mary's faith at the cross.

When we face our own suffering and perhaps our own death, we may remember the challenging words of Jesus to all who would be his disciples: "If any want to become my followers, let them deny themselves and take up their cross and follow me. For those who want to save their life will lose it, and those who lose their life for my sake, and for the sake of the gospel, will save it" (Mark 8:34b–35). As we face sufferings, we can also turn for strength to the figure of Mary at the cross. Hearing the words of Jesus and identifying with Mary, we might begin to come to terms with our own suffering, but we still will not understand it.

A spontaneous question in the face of suffering and death is "Why?" But the question is fundamentally unanswerable, at least here on earth, where we have only a partial view of life. The words of Jesus and the experience of Mary point us in another direction; we should not be asking why we suffer or where our suffering comes from, but rather where our suffering is leading us and what possibilities it is opening up for us. As we identify with Jesus and Mary in their experience of the cross, we find ourselves looking not to the past but to the future.

The Resurrection of Jesus

I n her journey of faith, Mary shared in the Easter experience, the resurrection of Jesus from the dead. There are no
passages in the Bible that describe exactly how she shared in
it, however. We can assume that since she was with him at his
birth, while she grew up, during his public ministry, and at his
death, she would also be with him in his rising from the dead.
Furthermore, we know that she was part of the community
of his disciples, the new family of God that Jesus had begun to
gather. It was in this community that the risen Jesus was
experienced.

Mary's faith was formed as a resurrection faith. Perhaps
the easiest way to understand this is to consider the earliest
statement of the faith of the Church: "Jesus is Lord!" When
the disciples made this profession of faith, they were referring
to Jesus and to the change he underwent at his resurrection.
The Jesus who walked with them and taught them and
healed them and gathered them was now the risen Lord. The
one who died the death of a common criminal on a cross was
now the Lord of life, the promised and hoped-for Messiah.
His journey and mission were not stopped by death; rather,
they found their fulfillment in his glorious rising from the dead.
He did not simply come back to life as if his resurrection were
a resuscitation.

Jesus' resurrection signaled total transformation, new and
glorious life. It became the unmistakable sign that the reign of
God had begun to take hold of our world. The old created

order that was subject to sin and death was passing away. An entirely new creation could be seen in his resurrection. Our longing for life in the face of death and our desire for freedom in the face of the slavery of sin find fulfillment and satisfaction beyond hope in the resurrection of Jesus. Because he is, as Paul said, "the firstborn within a large family" (Romans 8:29), he leads the human family through the cross to the new and utterly transformed life of glory in his resurrection. His rising is our hope. His rising belongs to us.

Like the other members of the community, Mary professed her belief in the Lordship of Jesus. Her son was now the risen Lord of life, the firstborn of the new creation. What she believed was expressed by Paul, who wrote about "the gospel concerning his Son, who was descended from David according to the flesh and was declared to be Son of God with power according to the spirit of holiness by resurrection from the dead, Jesus Christ our Lord" (Romans 1:3–4). As his mother, Mary knew better than anyone else his descent "from David according to the flesh." He was flesh from her flesh. Now she believed in him as "Son of God with power . . . by [his] resurrection from the dead." Her faith was once again intimately tied to her experience as the mother of Jesus. At the annunciation, she was asked to accept a child conceived by the Holy Spirit. At the resurrection, she was asked to believe in the new life of her son, and because of him in a new life in herself.

Like Mary, we are called to make a faith response. We believe in ourselves, our humanity, the gift of life created and given to us by God. At the same time, we believe that we have been drawn into the new and risen life of Jesus. As such, his life is transforming us; a new creation is taking place within us.

When Mary accepted the resurrection of Jesus, she was not looking at it as a confirmation of all that her son taught and did. The resurrection is more than a proof of what Jesus was about. It is that, but it is also much more. Mary's belief in the resurrection was a sign of her own participation in the new creation, the new life with God that was breaking into the world. Perhaps some comparisons with the world of nature can help us to understand her experience.

Winter in the Midwest is a long, dark, and cold season. Its severity makes the first signs of spring truly wonderful experiences. Watching the first crocus push its way up through the scarcely thawed soil makes you want to cheer. It may only amount to one of life's little breakthroughs, but it signals the arrival of a new season. New life is on the way. After seeing the ground blanketed in white for months, the pale green buds and the deep black soil are a novelty; it is like discovering color.

Spring also injects a new power, a new aliveness in the earth. The rush of water from melted snow, the energy felt in the warming rays of the sun, and the thunder of spring showers seem to awaken people and animals. Things are set in motion. Most of all, it seems, a long time of waiting is over; we have arrived. Even if we have lived through many springs, this one is different. It comes, as we had hoped, with its own colors and smells and sounds.

Experiencing the arrival of spring with its new life is a little like Mary's experience of her son's resurrection. For Mary, the resurrection of Jesus broke through the barriers of death. On Good Friday, she stood before the cross and what seemed to be the end of a dream, the collapse of possibilities. Easter passed beyond all boundaries and led her in faith into a new season of life. Mary now realized that Jesus was the Son of God in power. She knew him and continued to know him, but now in a new way as the risen one.

In the resurrection of Jesus, Mary also experienced the power of life over death, love over sin, and hope over despair. She found herself confirmed and renewed in her convictions about God's power and about the reversal of human expectations that are touched by God's power. Above all, in the resurrection of her son, Mary found the fulfillment of her hope. From the time of the annunciation onward, she let go of her own life. She had surrendered life only to have it given back to her in a measure far exceeding her hopes. Her hope had found its home.

Our experience of the resurrection of Jesus is less direct and less intense than that of Mary, yet we have some idea of what her discovery of new life in faith was like. We catch glimmers of what is to come in what has already begun. Every time we see life and love breaking through the limits of death-dealing forces and sin-enslaving powers, we touch the resurrection of Jesus. It may be the healing of body and soul, or the mending of broken relationships, or the establishment of peace. Whatever the form, the breakthrough puts us in touch with the presence of the risen Lord.

Every time we take a fresh look at things, recognizing the preciousness of life or the gifts of the earth or the talents of ourselves or others, we discover this world and its people in a new way. They are alive in God. Every time we sense a power for life and love at work, a power beyond our native abilities, we know the power of the risen Lord is touching our world. When, for example, people display remarkable energy in caring for the sick and the poor, in righting injustices, in creating art that reflects the beauty of the Creator, then we know the power of the risen Lord.

Every time people at life's end, or even before, give thanks for what has been and for God's merciful forgiveness of sin, they share at least in part the fulfillment of the promise contained in the resurrection of Jesus. We get a sense of arriving at the home of our promise, the fullness of life. In all these experiences, our journey of faith brings us to a reflection of our new life in the resurrection of Jesus. Our journey of faith enables us to proclaim with Mary, "Jesus is Lord!"

The Coming of the Holy Spirit

At the beginning of the Acts of the Apostles, we find a description of Jesus' ascension, his return to the Father after the resurrection and his great exaltation at the right hand of the Father. Then after the ascension, the followers of Jesus returned to Jerusalem where they prayed together and waited for the coming of the Holy Spirit, whom Jesus had promised. "All these were constantly devoting themselves to prayer, together with certain women, including Mary the mother of Jesus, as well as his brothers" (Acts 1:14).

Mary joined the other members of the new family of God, awaiting the coming of the Holy Spirit. They gathered in prayer. Then the Holy Spirit came upon them: "When the day of Pentecost had come, they were all together in one place. And suddenly from heaven there came a sound like the rush of a violent wind, and it filled the entire house where they were sitting. Divided tongues, as of fire, appeared among them, and a tongue rested on each of them. All of them were filled with the Holy Spirit. . ." (Acts 2:1–4).

Mary, who conceived Jesus by the power of the Holy Spirit, was now joined by that same Spirit to the followers of Jesus. The last picture we have of Mary in the Bible shows her gathered with the early Church in prayer. This is the link with ourselves. We are part of that Church gathered by the power of the Holy Spirit. In the Church, we are joined with

Mary; with her, we share a life and a journey of faith centered on her son and our Lord, Jesus Christ. With her, we join in constant prayer, offering to the Father our petitions, our praise, and our thanksgiving. With her, we declare, "I am the servant of the Lord," as we try to serve the world and one another.

We are the Church of faith, witness, prayer, and service. We are joined to one another, to all who are disciples of Jesus. In a unique way, we are joined to Mary, the mother of all disciples. We come to understand that the Church's journey of faith is a journey of faith with Mary. This journey is the subject of the second part of this book.

PART TWO

The Church's Journey of Faith with Mary

The Church's Journey of Faith with Mary

The Church's Journey of Faith with Mary

Marian Devotion

    Mary, the Mother of God

    Mary, the Virgin Mother of Jesus Christ

    The Immaculate Conception

    The Assumption

Marian Devotion

    The Communion of Saints

    Mary's Intercession

    Devotion and Devotions

    Apparitions of Mary

The Imitation of Mary: Mary as a Model

    Possibilities for Everyone Who Believes

    Possibilities for People in Particular
    Circumstances

"The understanding of Mary in Christian history unfolded along the lines of the Scriptures. The Church saw herself symbolized in the Virgin Mary. The story of Mary, as the Church had come to see her, is at the same time the record of the Church's own self-discovery."

Pastoral Letter, *Behold Your Mother*, 38

The Church's Journey of Faith with Mary

The travel industry—airlines, hotels, and car rentals—entice potential customers to take a trip by promising a good deal and, perhaps even more important, a snag-free journey. Even with stringent security measures, the unpredictability of weather, and tight scheduling, they try to make travel as painless as humanly possible. And, clearly, customers want and expect hassle-free travel. They do not want painful experiences *en route*. We are scarcely aware of how recent our expectations are for easy travel. Throughout most of history, travel meant a time-consuming venture that involved inconvenience and sometimes danger.

Traveling took time, energy, money, and the personal sacrifice of comfort. That is why making a pilgrimage, a journey to a holy place or shrine, was valued as a genuine act of religious devotion. The medieval pilgrim going to the Holy Land or to the shrine of Saint James the Apostle in Compostela, Spain, was given recognition for the undertaking. Making a pilgrimage signified a willingness to undergo hardship out of a sense of religious devotion.

The Second Vatican Council spoke of the Church as the pilgrim people of God. Keeping in mind the historical significance of pilgrimage, will help the reader understand what the council fathers meant. The Church as pilgrim people finds its motivation in faith; this faith enables and empowers the Church to begin and continue on its journey. The journey is through history, some two thousand years of it so far. It crosses mountains and valleys, desert land and fertile plains; there are moments of triumph and times of severe hardship. In other words, it is not a consistently easy kind of traveling.

Faith is the moving force and sustaining power of the journey, providing the Church with a vision of its destination and an assurance that the reign of God is taking hold of our world in Jesus Christ. The goal and the destination are tied to the person of Christ; his life, his mission, and his purpose give direction to the pilgrim journey of the Church in history. Consider the Church's journey as a process, as taking into itself more and more fully the unfolding mystery of Christ. But what precisely is the unfolding mystery of Christ? And how are we involved in it?

The phrase "mystery of Christ" may puzzle us since we usually associate a "mystery" either with something that is totally unknown or with detective novels. Obviously, the mystery of Christ has nothing to do with detective novels; in fact, it has little to do with the totally unknown. Saint Paul spoke about the mystery of Christ in this way: "[God] has made known to us the mystery of his will, according to his good pleasure that he set forth in Christ, as a plan for the fullness of time, to gather up all things in him, things in heaven and things on earth" (Ephesians 1:9–10).

The mystery, then, is a plan, and those who believe have been given an understanding of it. The goal is to bring everyone and everything under the one headship of Jesus Christ. Although the plan will come to completion "in the fullness of time," it is already unfolding in history.

The Church, as a community of people and as a movement, journeys through time and more and more deeply into the mystery of Christ. The Church experiences growth and development in understanding, feeling, and valuing. In statements of belief called doctrines, the Church expresses its growing understanding of the mystery of Christ. In prayer and devotion, it expresses its feelings and close attachment to that mystery. In living and behaving in a particular way, the Church expresses its value for the mystery of Christ, a value that leads it to action and ways of living. Doctrines, prayer and devotion, ways of living and behavior—these are the expressions of the Church's journey of faith as a pilgrim people.

The Church's journey of faith is the story of an unfolding relationship with God in the mystery of Christ. Since Christ is the starting point, the center, and the goal of this journey, we need to understand who he is for us. We can only do this in the measure that we come to terms with the links we have with him, the connections of the relationship. Among these connections or links, Mary has a preeminent and unique position; to understand Jesus Christ, we can do no better than try to understand Mary. In this sense, the Church has made a journey of faith with Mary. The Church has been on a pilgrimage with her, seeking deeper understanding and more affectionate feeling, embodying her lifestyle of faith.

This journey with Mary has found expression in various ways. The Church's understanding of Mary in relationship to Jesus has found expression in Marian doctrines, or statements of belief about Mary. The Church's cultivation of a sense of attachment to Mary in relationship to Jesus has found expression in numerous forms of prayer and devotion. The Church's way of embodying her faithful way of living centered on Jesus has found expression in the many ways it proposes Mary as a model of Christian living.

In the following pages, we will consider these different forms of expression of the Church's journey of faith with Mary. The first section treats the four major Marian doctrines: that she is the Mother of God; that she is ever virgin; that she was conceived without sin; that she was assumed into heaven. The second section is about Marian prayer and devotion—liturgical aspects will be discussed later in connection with the celebration of the feasts of Mary. The third section is about imitating Mary.

Marian Doctrines

The Church's journey of faith has involved a growing understanding of the mystery of Christ in the life and experience of Mary. This understanding has found expression in various doctrines, or statements of belief. In this section, I present and reflect upon the four major Marian doctrines: that Mary is the Mother of God; that she is ever virgin; that she was conceived immaculately; and that she was assumed into heaven.

Each doctrine is examined in four steps. First, I look at the doctrine as it is formulated in the traditional language of the Church. Since some of this language—such as virginal conception, immaculate conception, and assumption—does not belong to our everyday speech, I try to restate or even translate the doctrines into more comprehensible language. I also try to overcome the impression that the doctrines refer only to Mary. From my earlier reflections, we know that Mary's life and experience is closely and completely tied to that of Jesus, her Son, her Lord, and her Redeemer. In presenting the individual Marian doctrines, therefore, I point out their connection with and foundation in him.

The next perspective considers the history of the doctrine whenever that can help our understanding of it. If we recall that the Church is a pilgrim people on a journey of faith, then we should realize that understanding comes with time and experience. In this sense, we can say that doctrines develop with the Holy Spirit's guidance as expressions of our understanding of faith. The truth of a doctrine has always been present, but it takes time to understand and express the truth. This is nothing new. We have already seen that there were many things Mary did not understand at first; but she "treasured all these things in her heart" (Luke 2:51).

The Second Vatican Council, drawing on the experience of Mary and the experience of the Church itself over two thousand years, spoke of doctrinal development in this way: "This tradition which comes from the apostles develops in the Church with the help of the Holy Spirit. For there is a growth in the understanding of the realities and the words which have been handed down. This happens through the contemplation and study made by believers, who treasure these things in their hearts (cf. Luke 2:19, 51), through the intimate understanding of spiritual things they experience, and through the preaching of those who have received through episcopal succession the sure gift of truth. For, as the centuries succeed one another, the Church constantly moves forward toward the fullness of divine truth until the words of God reach their complete fulfillment in her" (*Dogmatic Constitution on Divine Revelation, 8*).

The third perspective looks at Scripture. Even though all the doctrines are not necessarily found directly in the Bible, all of them have biblical roots. Dwelling on certain passages in Scripture will help us arrive at a fuller appreciation of the particular doctrine under consideration.

The final perspective considers the possible effects of each doctrine on our own journey of faith. The doctrines are not merely curious bits of information about Mary and her relationship to Jesus. They do express unique privileges which belong to her alone because of her unique role in the story of redemption. Even so, these doctrines also tell us something about our lives too. It is important to know what effect they can have on our own journey of faith.

Mary, the Mother of God

I n the early centuries of Christianity, the Church had to wrestle with different ways of understanding and explaining who Jesus Christ is. The struggle involved much more than trying to piece together bits of information about Jesus. There were also personal considerations; the question was not simply who Jesus was in himself, but also who he is for us. If, for example, he were not truly God but simply a very good and holy human being, that would mean that our salvation would be in jeopardy. Only God can forgive sin; only God can offer us the fullness of life since he alone is the origin and destiny of all life.

In the end, only God can invite us to share his own life. If Jesus were merely a creature, the promise and offer of salvation contained in the gospels would be empty. If, on the other hand, Jesus were not truly human but simply had the appearance of a man, then our salvation would again be in jeopardy. The claim of the gospels is that he saved us by taking on our flesh, by being one like us in all things but sin. An inhuman or unhuman Jesus would not have touched humanity in a saving, healing, transforming way. For this reason, the controversies and the struggles of the early Church were very powerful in their impact on the community of faith. The controversies dealt with issues of deep importance for believers.

The Church gradually came to a clearer understanding of the person of Jesus Christ and to more exact expressions of that understanding. This occurred as bishops and theologians evaluated ideas that seemed to contradict the words of the Bible and the experience of the Church. At times, a given issue would come to a head. Then an ecumenical council, a meeting of bishops representing the entire Church, would be called together; it would propose carefully phrased doctrines, statements to be believed by the entire Church. The overall outcome of these councils was to affirm that Jesus Christ is true God and true man.

Jesus is true God or, in the technical language of the Council of Nicaea (A.D. 325), he is "consubstantial" with the Father. This means, according to the explanation of Saint Athanasius, one of the experts at that council, that everything in the Bible that is said of the Father can be said of the Son— except the name "Father." Jesus is therefore truly God. At the same time, he is truly human, a man "like us in all things but sin." In the language of the councils, which has become a part of the traditional language of the Church, we affirm that in Jesus Christ there is one person—the second person of the Trinity—with two natures, a human nature and a divine nature.

As one might suspect, controversies dealing with the humanity and the divinity of Jesus led to questions about his mother. The questions crystallized in a dispute about the titles of Mary. Nestorius, the patriarch of Constantinople and a theologian of some reputation, along with his followers, refused to call Mary *Theotokos*, the Greek word for "God bearer," or "mother of God." Since they believed that Christ

was *two* persons—a human person and a divine person—
joined into one, they insisted on calling Mary simply "mother
of Christ."

In A.D. 431, the Council of Ephesus affirmed that Mary is
truly the Mother of God. This means that she gave birth to
Jesus Christ in his humanity and that she contributed to the
formation of his humanity; but since he is one person, the
second person of the Trinity, the one she bore was God. By
approving "Mother of God" as Mary's title, the Council of
Ephesus affirmed and expressed the Church's faith about
Jesus Christ: that he is one person with two natures, human
and divine. (*Catechism of the Catholic Church*, 495, 509)

We are very much removed in time from the Council of
Ephesus, some fifteen hundred years to be exact. We may
also find ourselves removed from the concerns that sparked
the struggle surrounding the council. Perhaps the language of
the council seems strange and foreign to us. Nevertheless, the
declaration that Mary is the Mother of God has meaning for
us today. Recall for a moment the sense of the "Mystery of
Christ." It is God's plan to bring all things into one under
Christ's headship. Then recall that to understand the person
of Jesus Christ means to know how God has touched us and
how we can touch God. To affirm that Mary is the Mother of
God is to affirm the true humanity and the true divinity of
Jesus Christ and the unity of his person.

This affirmation also speaks to us about our relationship
with God and tells us that God reached out to us in Jesus
Christ on *our* terms, that is, in a human way. It says that our
reaching out to God in Jesus Christ is on *God's* terms, that is,

in a divine way. There is good news contained in this expression of faith. If we had fears and suspicions about the unbridgeable gap between God and ourselves, those fears and suspicions are now broken. Jesus Christ is the way of God to us. He is our way to God.

Earlier we said that it is not at all surprising that Mary is involved in questions about Jesus. She is the one who conceived him through the power of the Holy Spirit and brought him into our world. She was the link between his humanity and divinity. She stands as an eternal witness to the way that God calls the world into his own life of love. We might be tempted to think of religion as a philosophy of life that offers general principles, such as "Do good and avoid evil." Or we might think of religion as holding out some sort of vague promise that things will be better in the future. If this is the way we think, then all we have to do is look to Mary. She is not a general principle or a vague ideal. As the mother of God, she is evidence of the concreteness of God's plan for us in Jesus Christ.

The German Jesuit theologian Father Karl Rahner once remarked that abstractions do not have mothers. This may explain why the Church has kept Mary so prominently before itself in doctrines of faith and also in prayer and devotion. Cardinal Carlo Martini similarly has said: "Every time the Church becomes freshly aware of Mary's presence, there is a new burst of Christian life, with its accompanying strength, serenity, gracefulness and vivacity, precisely because we are taken back to the fundamental mysteries of the redemption." (*Ministers of the Gospel*, 1989, Crossroad, p. 92)

In her humanness and in her contribution to the humanity of Jesus, Mary is a constant reminder to the Church that its journey of faith draws it into a realm of personal relationships. This is very important for understanding the basic shape of our faith. We believe in the majesty and transcendence, or limitless greatness of God. In the book of Isaiah, the prophet speaking in the name of God says: "For my thoughts are not your thoughts, nor are your ways my ways, says the LORD. For as the heavens are higher than the earth, so are my ways higher than your ways and my thoughts than your thoughts" (Isaiah 55:8–9).

This could indicate a God who is unapproachable, with whom we cannot relate in any way; but that is not the case. We actually have a unique relationship with God. We do not relate to him as a chatty friend. Neither can we say that our relationship with him is bloodless, without feeling or even passion. The relationship is unique because our access to God is through the humanity of Jesus, the humanity he received from Mary, his mother. The possibilities for relating to God have become human possibilities in Jesus Christ.

Many passages in the Bible can help us understand Mary as the Mother of God. Perhaps one of the briefest references will be the most helpful: "But when the fullness of time had come, God sent his Son, born of a woman. . ." (Galatians 4:4). Mary is not even mentioned by name; she is simply referred to as a "woman." Still, the passage can trigger many thoughts as we recall the Church's struggle to understand its journey of faith with Mary.

When we hear about God's Son "born of a woman," our reaction should be one of amazement and wonder. Just think:

The Son of God has taken on our humanity; he has become one of us. The words at the beginning of John's Gospel echo in our ears: "And the Word became flesh and lived among us, and we have seen his glory, the glory as of a father's only son, full of grace and truth" (John 1:14).

As we dwell on the Word becoming flesh, God's Son being born of a woman, we should recall the mystery of every human birth, in which the creative, life-giving power of God is at work. It is true that there is only one Word of God. But there are many words of God, and we are among those words. We, too, have become flesh. We have shared the glory of the Son and the Father; we have been filled with their enduring love. Our opinion of humanity may sink low when we read or hear reports about war, robbery, rape, child abuse, and corruption of every sort. But even if we do not close our eyes to this inhumanity, and merely open our eyes to the humanity of the Word made flesh, "his Son, born of a woman," new prospects for this human race open up. This humanity can stand on holy ground. There is a possibility for us because God has not only touched our humanity but has also entered it.

Mary, the Virgin Mother of Jesus Christ

From the very beginning, the Church has proclaimed the profession of faith we find in the Apostles' Creed: He "was conceived by the Holy Spirit, born of the Virgin Mary." Unlike the title "Mother of God" or the doctrines of the Immaculate

Conception and the Assumption, there has been very little development in the Church's understanding of this doctrine. The central point, that Mary conceived and gave birth to Jesus as a virgin, has always been a part of the profession of faith. (See *Catechism of the Catholic Church*, 496–507, 510)

Technically, the doctrine is referred to as the virginal conception of Jesus. It states a biological fact: Jesus was not conceived in the ordinary way that human beings are conceived; he was conceived without a human father, by the power of the Holy Spirit. In the faith of the Church, Mary not only conceived and gave birth as a virgin, but she remained a virgin for the rest of her life. If we think about Mary's virginity simply as a biological fact, however, the doctrine of the virgin mother becomes a mere statement about an unusual birth. In fact, much more than biology is involved here. The doctrine signifies far more than a mere fact about someone, a fact that is removed from our lives and experiences. It is more than a curiosity that happens to be a part of the faith of the Church.

One way of going beyond the biological facts to a deeper understanding of this doctrine is to consider the way we think about birth today. A hospital keeps records of all the babies born there. An office of public records will provide a birth certificate upon request. Official documents, however, only attest to a biological event—to a birth. They merely establish a fact that is helpful when a person starts school, obtains a social security number, or wants a passport.

But records and certificates obviously do not tell the whole story; a birth is more than something that can be put down on paper. We celebrate a birthday because we want to recall not only the event of birth but also what the day of birth means. Our birth ushered us into life. It was a personal event that connected us with our origins in the love of two people. It was a personal event that led us into an entire world of relationships and possibilities. Our birth was a biological event, a fact of nature; but we can never consider ourselves mere products of a biological process. Neither can we consider the virginal conception and birth of Jesus as mere biological events.

Faith in Mary's virginal conception of Jesus has been as constant and steady in the Church as the countless times that believers have called on her as the Blessed Virgin Mary. Just as we think beyond the biological facts when we think of our own conception and birth, so, too, believers acknowledge more than an exception to a biological process in calling Mary the Blessed Virgin. Reading the scriptural account, the Church reflects on its experience of God's love shown in the mystery of Christ. In the virginal conception and birth of Jesus, the believing community recognizes the power and initiative of God who begins and brings about the plan of our salvation. The virginal conception and birth show clearly that Jesus is of God, that what he represents as God's outreach to humanity comes as a pure gift. It also shows that the destiny of Jesus is tied to our own.

Considering Mary as the virgin mother should lead us to incorporate Mary's experience into our own journey of faith. This is meant for all mothers, fathers, single people, as well as those in religious life and the priesthood who have committed themselves to celibate chastity. Sharing Mary's experience as the virgin mother means more than imitating a biological reality. It means sharing in what her virginity signifies for the Christian life.

As virgin, Mary is a sign of human poverty. She was not only materially poor; she also gave up many of the securities we associate with family life. Our own poverty may take on a different form; but to be in touch with our lack of resources and the things we depend upon is to be in touch with the reality of who we are. As virgin, Mary is also a sign of solitude. She knew what it meant to be alone. Again, our own solitude may take on a different form; but there is a radical kind of aloneness that belongs to each one of us, married or unmarried, living on a desert island or in a large city. Our acceptance of solitude means accepting who we are.

Finally, as virgin, Mary is a sign of openness to God. Her life was not predetermined; she was a person open to possibilities, specifically the possibilities that God offered her. To accept our own openness may mean looking beyond what we consider dead ends and determined paths, recognizing that there are possibilities offered by God that go beyond our imagining. When we acknowledge our lack of resources, when we are alone, when we are open to God's offer, the Lord can move in our lives.

The Immaculate Conception

In 1854, Pope Pius IX solemnly proclaimed the doctrine of the Immaculate Conception. It states that Mary was conceived without the stain of original sin. What does this mean? Some may wonder about the meaning of the phrase "stain of original sin"; others about the very purpose of the doctrine. Does it really make a difference? And why did it take the Church so long to solemnly proclaim the

Immaculate Conception as something that Catholics are to believe?

To answer these questions, we will begin with the idea of original sin. Then we will look at the development of the doctrine; its history will help us understand its meaning. Finally, with this background, we will be in a position to see that the doctrine of the Immaculate Conception does make a difference and that it has an effect on our lives today.

Perhaps the easiest way to understand original sin is to look at our own experience of sin. All of us are born in need of God's grace. The Second Vatican Council pointed to the very human experience we have of feeling divided within ourselves: "Examining his heart, man finds that he has inclinations toward evil. . . . (He) is split within himself" (*Pastoral Constitution on the Church in the Modern World*, 13). We all experience the struggle between good and evil. Even Saint Paul experienced an inner division. He wrote: "I do not understand my own actions. For I do not do what I want, but I do the very thing I hate" (Romans 7:15).

The condition into which we are born seems to be a lack of wholeness. We are born with a sense of not being at home with ourselves or our world or God. We stand in need of God's grace. In other words, being born does not automatically put us in a loving relationship with God. Traditionally, the way of expressing this is to say that original sin formally consists in a lack of sanctifying grace. (See the *Catechism of the Catholic Church*, 396–421)

As we think about original sin as a part of our experience, we ought to remember that we are not talking about personal sin. *Sin* as used in *original sin* has a special sense. We are not talking about the exercise of our own freedom that distances and alienates us from God and from one another—that is personal sin. Rather, we are talking about being born into a situation of alienation, of not-at-homeness with God, before we make any particular decisions.

We are born needy. More specifically, we are born in need of a relationship with Jesus Christ the Savior, who breaks down the distance and the alienation between God and ourselves. Jesus heals and reconciles the divisions we experience within ourselves. He links us with our God and with one another.

With this understanding of original sin, we can return to the declaration of the doctrine made by Pope Pius IX in 1854. The decree reads: "From the first moment of her conception, the Most Blessed Virgin Mary by a unique grace and privilege of God and in view of the merits of Jesus Christ, the savior of the human race, was preserved from all stain of original sin." This statement of the Church is the outcome of many years of reflection, prayer, and consideration. (See *Catechism of the Catholic Church*, 490–493, 508)

Although belief in the Immaculate Conception was a part of the Church's faith for many centuries, some theologians as great as Saint Thomas Aquinas could not accept the doctrine *as it was proposed in their time*. The principal reason for their rejection of the doctrine was that they were not certain whether the doctrine as proposed held that Mary did not need to be redeemed. Did she not, indeed, need the saving and healing power of her son?

Although the Church had always held Mary in very high regard, that did not necessarily mean that she did not fall under the influence of original sin. She belonged after all to the human family and would therefore need the saving work of Christ. The breakthrough came when theologians recognized that even though Mary needed redemption, she was redeemed in a unique way. *We are saved* or redeemed from original sin when we are baptized and make our profession of faith in Jesus Christ. *Mary was saved* or redeemed by being preserved from original sin from the very moment of her conception.

If the doctrine of the Immaculate Conception means that Mary enjoyed a special privilege, what is its meaning for us? Does it have any connection with our own lives? In fact, it does; the Church's journey of faith with Mary that led to the proclamation of the doctrine has a close connection with our experience. The way God moved in Mary's life from the very first moment of her conception is similar to the way he moves in our lives. The Church's journey of faith with Mary brings us to a deeper understanding of the way God works in our lives.

The doctrine of the Immaculate Conception says that Mary is who she is because of a gift of God. She is holy, not because of her own merits, not because of something that she earned; she is holy because God loved her. She was drawn close to God by God himself; she did not draw herself close to him. Since she received God's favor from "the first moment of her conception," there can be no doubt that the responsibility for who she was rested with God.

Mary's Immaculate Conception reflects and proclaims the absolute primacy of God's grace in human life. Something similar also happens in our own lives. In Christian faith terms, there are no self-made people. Everything depends on a gift of God. In other words, God's grace is absolutely primary and foundational for us.

The doctrine of the Immaculate Conception also states that Mary enjoyed a "unique grace." She was indeed a person of privilege; we do not share her unique gift. Does this mean, then, that her privilege of being conceived without sin distances her from us instead of bringing her more closely into our lives? Not at all. Her relationship with God is not merely a question of personal privilege. Mary belongs to the human family. This is an association that is unbreakable.

Because Mary belongs to our family, she stands with us. She also stands for us, for the human family. Mary's personal holiness, which was a gift of God, made it possible for her to accept and cooperate with God's saving outreach in Jesus. She did all this not simply for herself but as one of us and for all of us. The fourteenth-century English mystic Julian of Norwich put it this way: "Look on Mary and see how you are loved."

In its journey of faith, the Church follows the example of Mary who "treasured all these things in her heart" (Luke 2:51). Over the course of many centuries, the Church took the words of the Bible about Mary and held them in its memory, considering them in light of the experience of the mystery of Christ. This journey led the Church in 1854 to officially proclaim the doctrine of the Immaculate Conception. Particular words from Luke's gospel played an important part in the Church's prayerful reflection,

"Greetings, favored one! [full of grace] The Lord is with you" (Luke 1:28).

As we consider these words and see our own experience in Mary's, we come to the basic understanding that God's gift is primary in our lives. God's gift is his presence—"The Lord is with you." God's presence empowers and enables us from within, as it did for Mary, to take up the call of our lives and respond generously. The understanding that God's gift is primary in our lives quite naturally leads us to a feeling of gratitude. Our response should be one of grateful living as we contemplate the greatness of the gift that has been given to us.

The Assumption

The Assumption is the most recently defined Marian doctrine. In 1950, Pope Pius XII solemnly proclaimed: "The immaculate and ever-virgin Mary, Mother of God, was assumed body and soul into the glory of heaven when her life on earth was completed." (*Catechism of the Catholic Church*, 966–974) The language of the doctrine, especially the word "assumed," might be a barrier to our understanding since in everyday speech to *assume* means "to take for granted." The language of the doctrine, however, was borrowed from the Latin, in which the word for assumed means "taken up." But aside from translating the language, there are deeper questions concerning the sense and meaning of the doctrine. Once again, looking at our experience and current situation in faith will help us find the answers.

We can accurately say that as pilgrim people we live in an in-between time. According to Saint Paul, Jesus is the Amen to all God's promises: "For in him every one of God's promises is a 'Yes' " (2 Corinthians 1:20). His life, death, and resurrection signal the breaking through of the reign of God into our lives. God's plan was begun in Jesus Christ and will be brought to completion; the mystery, God's plan, is now unfolding.

Our experience in life, however, plainly tells us that we have not yet arrived. We are a pilgrim people, a people on the way, not a people who have arrived. All we need to do is glance at the daily newspaper to find countless signs of humanity's lack of completeness and wounds of brokenness. As long as there are hungry people, innocent people caught in wars, children exploited by greed, and people killing each other, death-dealing forces exercise their power.

We do not even need to look at a newspaper to find a lack of completeness and an experience of brokenness. Our own lives and the lives of people close to us bear the marks and bruises of destructive forces. When there is misunderstanding in families, sickness in our bodies or minds, the threat of death, and the failure to live up to the moral demands of the Gospel, we know with the cool eye of realism that we have not yet arrived.

The doctrine of the Assumption declares that one member of our human family, Mary, has arrived. She now enjoys what we hope for. Mary, in other words, anticipates even now the full destiny that will be ours someday. She is totally changed, body and soul; she has been fully drawn into the life of God.

As we begin to understand the doctrine of the Assumption, we may wonder how Mary has been transformed, or changed. What does it mean to experience the fullness of redemption? These are very good questions, but they are unanswerable. Our capacity to understand is very much limited by our present experience. In our earthly state of existence, we cannot appreciate the full sense and shape of the transformation that Mary enjoys and we await.

Like Paul, we know there is a difference, but we have no idea of the details; we can only rely on feeble comparisons. The people of the Church of Corinth asked Paul, "How are the dead raised? With what kind of body do they come?" He answered them with comparisons drawn from nature: "So it is with the resurrection of the dead. What is sown is perishable, what is raised is imperishable. It is sown in dishonor, it is raised in glory. It is sown in weakness, it is raised in power. It is sown a physical body, it is raised a spiritual body" (1 Corinthians 15:35, 42–44).

Although belief in the Assumption was a part of the Church's faith for many centuries, the doctrine was not solemnly declared until 1950. Obviously, the Church's journey of faith in coming to understand and affirm the Assumption of Mary had a long history. As we have already seen, something similar happened with the doctrine of the Immaculate Conception. Over the centuries, the Church reflected on its own experience and contemplated the mystery of Christ and how it works itself out in history. After prayerful reflection, the Church formulated its understanding of the privileged position of Mary. At the heart of its understanding is a central conviction: that God's reign has already broken into our lives.

The fullness of life is not only a promise and possibility, but it has already begun to take hold of our world, to take hold of the human family.

If we want to dwell in prayer and reflection on Mary's Assumption, many passages of the Bible suggest themselves for our use. One passage does so with particular force; it is the earliest confession of faith in the Christian community: "Jesus is Lord!" Contained in this brief statement of belief is the strong and joyful affirmation that Jesus is the risen one, that he is the Lord of life. He lives, and his life-giving Spirit is at work among us even now, drawing us into the fullness of life. To affirm that Mary is assumed into heaven is to reaffirm that Jesus is Lord, that he is the risen one who as the Lord of life draws everyone to himself. Mary fully shares in the resurrection of her son.

Our life of faith is a "life on the way." We hold to a hope. This is what enables and empowers us to make the journey with all its difficulties. To exercise such a power in our lives, however, hope has to be more than a word or an ideal; it must take shape as a personalized event. We need the experience of a person with whom we can identify. This is precisely the empowerment of hope through faith that we have when we affirm Mary's Assumption. We pin our hope, our future, on what God in Christ has already done among us—in Mary.

Marian Devotion

A fter tracing Mary's journey of faith in part one, we began to consider the Church's journey of faith with Mary. We have just reflected on the Church's understanding of Mary in the mystery of Christ. Since a faith journey involves feelings, values, attitudes, emotions, and understanding, however, we will now turn our attention to the Church's attachment to and union with Mary. This can be seen in its experience of Mary's intercession, which we will consider in the context of the communion of saints.

The Communion of Saints

I n the very last part of the Apostles' Creed, we profess: "I believe in the Holy Spirit, the holy catholic Church, the communion of saints, the forgiveness of sins, the resurrection of the body, and life everlasting." Sometimes, the formulas we repeat become like old friends—we take them for granted, but don't necessarily understand them. This may be the case with the communion of saints. We accept it, we profess it, but we may not understand it.

What precisely is the communion of saints? A communion is a group of people who are united and have something in common. They may be united in conviction or feeling or values. In the communion of saints, the union happens on all three levels: a common faith, a common love, and a common sense of what is important binds people together. It should be noted that the people who are bound together are called saints. In other words, they have been or are being made holy in Jesus Christ.

By the power of the Holy Spirit, the saints find their deepest communion in sharing God's life. (See *Catechism of the Catholic Church*, 946–962.) The saints are not only outstanding individuals who have been canonized, that is, recognized as holy by the Church in an official way. They also include those who are not canonized but who are with the Lord, as well as people like ourselves who are making their pilgrim way upon this earth.

Another way to look at the communion of saints is to consider it as the new family of God gathered together in the mystery of Christ by the power of the Holy Spirit. This comes close to the idea of Saint Paul: "So then you are no longer strangers and aliens, but you are citizens with the saints and also members of the household of God. . ." (Ephesians 2:19). Simply put, the communion of saints is the family of God. God lives in it, as well as those who live in God; a life of presence—God to us and us to God—links the saints together as one family.

To belong to the communion of saints means to belong to one another and to live in a bond of unity with one another. This bond, which is a union in faith, hope, and love, does not lessen what we are as individuals. In fact, each person in the communion of saints is called individually and uniquely to this "life in communion." Some are called to play special roles, however. In the Bible, we find examples of individuals called for a special task, individuals who stand for the whole people while still standing with their people. Abraham, who is our father in faith, stood at the head of the chosen people and accepted with them and for them the covenant that God offered. Similarly, Moses stood for and with his people as he accepted the covenant of Sinai. In the communion of saints, Mary is that kind of person. She stands for and with the people of God as the new and everlasting covenant in Jesus Christ unfolds.

The communion of saints, then, brings out a basic conviction of our faith: Our lives are linked together. Who we are and what we do—whether it be good or evil—has an effect on the entire people to which we belong. There is no such thing as a private sin or a private act of virtue. Everything is connected. As Saint Paul said: "For just as the body is one and has many members, and all the members of the body, though many, are one body, so it is with Christ. . . . If one member suffers, all suffer together with it; if one member is honored, all rejoice together with it" (1 Corinthians 12:12, 26).

Mary's Intercession

Our reflection on the communion of saints brings us to an important conclusion: We make the journey of faith together. With this in mind, we will now consider the Church's experience of Mary's intercession. Mary journeys with the Church, is linked with us, and has an effect on us. (See *Catechism of the Catholic Church*, 967–970, 975, 2673–2679, 2682.)

The word "intercession" does not belong to our everyday vocabulary, but the idea behind it is quite simple. It means praying on behalf of someone else; in this case, Mary praying on behalf of us. Mary is viewed as a mediatrix or go-between, a person of power whose patronage we seek, a loving mother who offers protection. We pray and ask her to pray for us. People sometimes wonder, however, why we pray in this roundabout way. Why not offer our prayers directly to God? Why even pray? If we ask God for something, is his mind changed by our prayer? Is Mary able to change God's mind? And what does this do to the role of Jesus? Does he lose his central position?

Let us begin with the question about Jesus' role. Any talk of intercession or mediation connected with Mary or the saints must be understood in such a way that it does not take away from the unique position and mission of Jesus Christ. This was made clear by the fathers of the Second Vatican Council: "Mary cares for the brethren of her Son. . . . Therefore the Blessed Virgin is invoked by the Church under the titles of Advocate . . . and Mediatrix. These, however, are to be so understood that they neither take away from nor add anything to the dignity and efficacy of Christ the one Mediator" (*Dogmatic Constitution on the Church*, 62).

In making this statement of principle, the council fathers followed the biblical teaching that Jesus is the only mediator: "For there is one God; there is also one mediator between God and humankind. . ." (1 Timothy 2:5). All intercession, including that of Mary, must be connected with his. After tracing Mary's journey of faith, we know in fact that all that she is and does has its origin in her son.

Another question about prayer, specifically prayer of petition, or prayer that asks for something, remains to be answered. Prayers of praise and thanksgiving are easy to understand. In fact, we would be ungrateful if we did not offer such prayers. But prayers of petition are different; they could be interpreted as attempts to bring God down to a human level. Do our prayers of petition change God's mind about things? If we pray for someone's health, will recovery from an illness take place because of our prayer? If we pray for a safe journey, will we arrive safely because of the prayer? Put that way, the questions cannot be answered directly. We cannot speak of "changing God's mind" because that would put him on a human level. We cannot pinpoint the exact effect of our prayers for health or a safe journey because so many different factors contribute to the healing of an illness and to safety. These questions, however, should make us more aware and should lead us to reflect on our experience of prayer.

What happens in prayer is that we identify with God, and God identifies with us; a marriage of two wills, God's will and our will, takes place. We cannot think of the prayer of petition in terms of a child tugging on a parent's sleeve asking for candy. There is a kind of willfulness in that request—the child is trying to "get something" out of the parent. In the prayer of petition we are not or should not be trying willfully to "get something" out of God. Rather, we should be trying to get in touch with the will of the one who loves us, who makes all things work for the good of those who love him.

By the same token, we let God who loves us get in touch with our will. This can be seen clearly in the petition contained in the Lord's prayer, "Thy kingdom come." This is the overarching petition of all our prayers, that the reign of God will come and take hold of us. When "Thy kingdom come" is prayed from the heart, a marriage of two wills takes place; we identify with God, and God identifies with us. Our cause is affirmed as God's cause, and God's cause is affirmed as our cause.

With this basic understanding of the prayer of petition, we can return to our consideration of Mary's intercession. Consider the popularity of the Hail Mary. Look at the thousands of people who make pilgrimages to centers of Marian devotion, such as Lourdes, Fatima, Loreto, and our own National Shrine of the Immaculate Conception. At these centers and elsewhere, people offer particular petitions for healing, or peace, or safety. These prayers, offered through Mary's intercession, express our life together in the communion of saints. We make the journey of faith together and affect one another in the journey.

We call upon Mary and she prays for us. But her power as intercessor actually belongs to Jesus, her son and our great intercessor before the Father. Her intimate connection with him not only in her physical motherhood but in her faith is the source of her power. In the communion of saints, we too share his power. Jesus makes this assurance in John's gospel: "Very truly, I tell you, the one who believes in me will also do the works that I do and, in fact, will do greater works than these, because I am going to the Father. I will do whatever you ask in my name, so that the Father may be glorified in the Son" (John 14:12–13).

One other point should be stressed. If we pray with Mary and through her intercession, then we must follow through in her style of faith and prayer. As we saw when we considered the Annunciation, Mary was totally open to God's initiative, but she also accepted the responsibility of God's call with its costs and demands. There are practical, social, and sometimes even political implications attached to our prayers of petition. We cannot pray for health without taking the ordinary means of maintaining or restoring health. Prayers for health, in other words, do not take away our need for medicine and medical care. We cannot pray for peace without getting involved in the structures and systems that contribute to peace. Prayer is not genuine if we pray in a detached and passive way, waiting for something to happen. This would be a denial of our belief that we are created and redeemed in freedom, that we are responsible for our lives and the world.

Devotion and Devotions

The Church's journey of faith with Mary has included more than a journey leading to the formulation of doctrines. The faith journey of the Church also reaches into the very human dimension of feelings, especially feelings of being attached or united. We have already begun to explore this aspect of the Church's journey of faith with Mary in terms of the communion of saints and Mary's intercession. Now, we turn our attention to the idea and experience of devotion and devotions. (See *Catechism of the Catholic Church*, 971.)

By the word "devotion" we mean the overall feeling of attachment that people have toward Mary. Although our primary concern here is Mary, the word has been applied in a similar way to the relationship people have with Jesus and the saints. "Devotions," on the other hand, refers primarily to various kinds of religious practices, especially on a personal level. We will consider both "devotion" and "devotions" to understand their meaning and how they connect with the Church's journey of faith.

The word "devotion" comes from the Latin verb *sese devovere*, meaning "to commit oneself," or "to vow oneself." Our own experience of devotion agrees with the idea of commitment. Being devoted to someone or something means committing yourself to a person or cause or ideal. But devotion involves more than commitment; it usually carries with it a sense of attachment.

Perhaps the best way to understand devotion, then, is to see it as committed attachment. Because it involves commitment, devotion implies some personal investment on our part. Because it involves attachment, devotion includes feelings, especially feelings of closeness.

In everyday speech we might refer to something, such as our work, as the object of our devotion. For example, we might say that a scientist is devoted to his or her work. Our primary and fundamental experience of devotion, however, draws us into the world of persons. We are devoted to people with whom we are united by feelings of attachment; our commitments of loyalty and faithfulness are directed to people. Devotion speaks of a world of persons because devotion results from our intimacy with others. Good friends are devoted to each other because they recognize their closeness, their intimacy with one another. They share a history of experiences together, and their feelings for one another are mutual.

To complete our understanding of devotion, we need to add one more very important element to its description. Devotion cannot and does not stay locked inside of us; it is not merely an inner experience. Devotion necessarily finds ways of expressing itself. Gift giving, for example, speaks of the value we hold in the other person. A bouquet of flowers, a box of candy, or a book speaks in the name of the giver about the committed attachment that is felt, the devotion that exists for the other person.

Sometimes the expression of devotion finds a more direct means, as in the unambiguous message "I love you," or in nicknames that people give each other. Whatever the means, devotion to another person will find a way of expressing itself. This is what happens in the Church; devotion to Mary finds a way of expressing itself. And these expressions are referred to as devotions.

Although devotions to Mary have varied widely according to time, place, and culture, they all express the same under- lying sense of committed attachment. During the Middle Ages, craftsmen built the cathedral of Notre Dame in Paris, Our Lady's church. We can picture the famous Michelangelo sculpting the *Pietà*, or the numerous anonymous monk artists of the Eastern Church painting icons of Mary. Flowers are gathered in May for Mary's altars; her statues are crowned with flowers. In Mexico City, a steady stream of pilgrims approaches the great basilica of Our Lady of Guadalupe on their knees. Colorful processions take place in Italy and Spain. Hymns and songs are composed and sung in Mary's honor. Candles are lit, banners are unfurled, and money offerings made—all for her. A direct expression of devotion comes in various prayers and prayer forms, such as novenas, litanies, and the rosary.

There are many kinds of devotions as there are many languages and dialects, skin colors, and ways of dressing. Their specific shape varies widely according to different cultures, different periods of history, and individual temperaments. The variety follows naturally from the differences that make our lives interesting. Devotion in southern Europe will differ from that in northern Europe. African culture will create its own forms of devotion. The medieval will not always be suitable for the twenty-first century. This variety, or pluralism, is not only a necessity, it is a very good thing.

Obviously, we cannot look upon all forms of Marian devotion uncritically. We have to be certain that they are sound and genuine expressions of the Church's faith. In order to do this, an individual devotion has to be judged in the light of specific values. This can be done by asking a few questions. They are important because the Church's approval of a devotion and our participation in it depends on how the questions are answered.

The first question concerns the way a particular form of Marian devotion meets the people of a specific time and place. Is this devotion and its expression suitable to the people of this time and place and background? The people of an upper-middle-class American parish, for example, might not find a picture of Mary done in a sentimental nineteenth-century artistic style a suitable expression of their devotion. By the same token, the people of a rural Latin American Indian parish might not find a modern abstract representation of Mary a suitable expression of their devotion. Different cultures inspire different artistic representations.

The second question aims to determine whether or not a devotion to Mary is in harmony with the total life of Christian faith. In other words, does it keep the mystery of Jesus Christ at the center? Does it draw its origin from and return to the Father's plan to bring all things under the headship of Jesus Christ? Any form of Marian devotion that eclipses or over-shadows Jesus in favor of Mary is untrue to the core of our faith and certainly untrue to Mary's own faith.

A third and final question concerns the relationship between a Marian devotion and the liturgy, the public worship of the Church. Although we will consider Mary in the liturgy in greater detail in part three, we can anticipate some of our concerns with the following question: Does the particular form of Marian devotion we are evaluating harmonize with and lead to the liturgical life of the Church, particularly to the celebration of the Eucharist and the other sacraments?

The Church's journey of faith is a journey of worship, and Mary joins with the Church in remembering and celebrating the death and resurrection of her son. A life of devotion to Mary that forgets or displaces the central prayer of the entire Church is not true to the very style of Mary's life.

These questions aim to discover whether a Marian devotion is worthy of our acceptance and participation. Sometimes, Church authorities arrive at a negative conclusion about a particular form of devotion. But in general the Church finds itself confirmed in its journey of faith with Mary through the wide range of devotions that have developed over time and in many places and cultures.

Apparitions of Mary

For some Catholics devotion to Mary is connected with apparitions. Mary is said to have appeared at various places, especially during the past 150 years or so. The appearances, as reported, are frequently made to children and are often connected with a message or appeal, usually a call to prayer and penance. Among the best-known apparitions are the ones that took place at Lourdes in France, Knock in Ireland, and Fatima in Portugal. The shrines erected at these sites, as well as at other places where apparitions have taken place, draw countless visitors who come to pray, express their devotion, and perhaps seek a favor through Mary's intercession.

The stories of Mary's appearances raise two questions: Did the apparitions really happen? And if so, what do they mean and how do they tie in to the larger picture of the Church's faith? The Church has proceeded cautiously in these matters, neither uncritically accepting all stories of apparitions as true nor quickly discounting the possible expressions of genuine faith connected with them. We would do well to proceed with the same caution.

One fact is very important for understanding the Church's position on the various apparitions of Mary: Apparitions belong to what is called *private revelation*; they stand in contrast to *public revelation*. This point needs further explanation. Public revelation refers to God's action of making himself and his intentions known to the human family. The fathers of the Second Vatican Council spoke of public revelation this way: "By this revelation then, the deepest truth about God and the salvation of man is made clear to us in Christ, who is the Mediator and at the same time the fullness of all revelation" (*Dogmatic Constitution on Divine Revelation*, 2).

Our faith, professed when we proclaim the creed and affirmed when we submit our intellect and will to what God has revealed, is our response to God's revelation. We believe what God has revealed; we accept and trust what God has shown us about himself in Jesus Christ. To speak of public revelation, then, means to speak of what God makes known for all people to believe. We come in touch with this revelation through the written word of Scripture as well as in the living word of the Church's tradition. *Public* in public revelation means that which is destined for everyone in every age.

Private revelation is altogether different. Since Jesus is the Amen to all God's promises, since he is the complete and final word of the Father, there is no question of private revelations adding anything to our knowledge of God and his ways. The opening of the letter to the Hebrews puts it this way: "Long ago God spoke to our ancestors in many and various ways by the prophets, but in these last days he has spoken to us by a Son. . ." (Hebrews 1:1–2). Private revelations can develop some aspect of the mystery of Jesus Christ or redirect us to him. They can never change the core of what God has spoken in Jesus, however, or the core of our faith response to God's revelation.

Besides recognizing what private revelations are not, we can also look on them in more positive terms. Private revelations represent the spiritual experiences of particular individuals. They are experiences in which others can share and perhaps find some benefit, especially in a given historical moment. Private revelations or the special spiritual experiences of individuals can therefore direct us to the core of our faith in Jesus Christ. There is never an obligation to believe in these private revelations. We are free to believe them or not. (See *Catechism of the Catholic Church*, 67.)

As previously noted, the Church deals cautiously with apparitions since they are considered private revelations. When Church officials examine the devotions relating to an apparition of Mary, they do so for a very specific and limited purpose. They do not attempt to prove or disprove the genuineness of a particular appearance of Mary, that is, try to establish scientifically what exactly occurred in an alleged apparition of Mary. This would be a very difficult task since the apparition belongs to the personal spiritual experience of individuals and not to the core of the Church's faith. Rather, they look to the style and quality of devotion that is generated by the apparition.

When the Church finally gives its approval, it makes a limited statement. It says that the prayers and devotions attached to a particular apparition, as well as the shrine or center of the devotion, are genuine expressions of faith. In other words, the approval means that the devotions practiced in a given shrine associated with an apparition are in harmony with the fuller life of the Church's faith. The Church may also confirm the spiritual benefit or usefulness of the message connected with the apparition for the Christian life. The message of Fatima, for example, to pray for peace, is a spiritually relevant and important message for our time.

The Imitation of Mary: Mary as Model

We have considered the Church's journey of faith in coming to a fuller and deeper understanding of Mary in light of the mystery of Christ.

The Church's journey of faith, however, involves more than growing in its understanding of Mary or in its feelings of attachment to her. It also involves developing a sense of value about Mary that can open possibilities for daily living. In other words, because the Church values Mary as a woman of great faith, and as the mother of all Jesus' disciples, it recognizes that she is worthy of being imitated. This means that we look upon Mary as a model person in the family of faith. She embodied what believing in Jesus Christ is all about and expressed that belief in her life and her action. She is, therefore, the great example of holiness. (See *Catechism of the Catholic Church*, 2030.)

Mary and the saints serve as models for living out the mystery of Christ. God's plan to bring all things under the headship of Christ unfolds in Jesus' life, teaching, death, and resurrection. Although the mystery of Christ is one, there are countless possibilities for living it out, possibilities that vary with time, place, culture, and personal temperament. In fact, the history of the Church is the story of a people journeying in faith and realizing the many possibilities for living out the one mystery of Christ.

Mary's position in the Church is, of course, unique. As the mother of Jesus and as a woman of great faith, she has been a model of faith-filled living and has inspired countless possibilities for people of faith across the centuries. We will consider the possibilities she offers under two general headings: the possibilities for everyone who believes, and the possibilities for people in particular life circumstances.

Possibilities for Everyone Who Believes

M ary shows the possibilities of faithful living for everyone who believes. These possibilities flow from her openness to God and poverty of spirit, which made her responsive to the movement of God in her life. Mary accepted God's call freely and with a sense of her own responsibility; she realized the price of accepting that call. Her call led her beyond herself in loving service. She plainly showed how faith gives birth to love. She bore her child, watched him grow, followed him in his ministry, attentively listened to his words.

In her life with Jesus during his early years and public ministry, Mary gave the example of watchful faith, a faith that detects the action of God in the events of life. She followed Jesus to the cross and in his resurrection. She made the passage with him from death to life through her hope. She proclaimed the greatness of the Lord, and so was at the beginning of the great mission of evangelization, which continues in our own day. In her poverty of spirit, faithfulness, trust, love, watchful faith, clear proclamation of the good news, and undying hope, Mary showed possibilities for all of us who make the journey of faith.

Possibilities for People in Particular Circumstances

L ike us, Mary lived her life in a particular set of circumstances. She was a Jewish woman living in Palestine during the first century. She was a virgin, a wife, and a mother. Eventually, she belonged to the group of disciples, or followers of Jesus, who believed in him and lived by his Spirit. The example of Mary's life has provided believers with possibilities for their own journey of faith, especially when they can identify with her in their particular life situation.

Mary as a virgin is the sure sign of the believer who lives from God's gift and no other resource. It was only through God's initiative that she was able to be life-bearing and life-giving. Mary as virgin has been a model for people who live a vowed religious life: sisters, monks, brothers, and priests; she opens to them possibilities for faithful living. As they journey in faith, they want to live out their commitment to the mystery of Christ in a transparent way. Like Mary, they want everyone to know that they live by God's initiative and that in this way they are enabled to be life-bearing and life-giving.

Mary as a mother gave her son flesh. She took care of him as he grew up, and contributed to the formation of his full humanity. As a mother, Mary has been and continues to be a model for parents. She opens possibilities for those who live out their faith commitment in life-giving and nurturing ways. She shows parents a way of looking on the life they bring into the world as something more than a product of themselves; she invites them to see that the life they hold is already held by God. They are to treasure this life, love it, nurture it—but they can never claim it absolutely for themselves. Mary shows parents how to follow the lives of their children as, in an exemplary way, she followed the ministry, death, and resurrection of Jesus. Through association with Mary, fathers and mothers can become better parents because they live by faith.

Throughout the public life of Jesus and after the Ascension, Mary belonged to the community of disciples. As a member of the Church—those gathered in faith, evangelizing witness, prayer, and service—she is an example of all who live an experience of church. As we gather in faith for prayer, witness, and service, she serves as our model. Her presence and faithfulness to Jesus and her participation in the life of the Church point the way for all who share in the life of the Church.

PART THREE

The Church Celebrates the Feasts of Mary

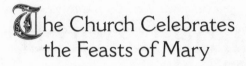

The Church Celebrates the Feasts of Mary

The Church Celebrates the Feasts of Mary

The Immaculate Conception: December 8

Our Lady of Guadalupe, Patroness of the Americas: December 12

Mary, the Mother of God: January 1

The Annunciation: March 25

The Visitation: May 31

The Assumption: August 15

The Birth of Mary: September 8

*"When Mary is honored, her son is duly acknowl-
edged, loved and glorified, and His commandments
are observed. To venerate Mary correctly means to
acknowledge her Son, for she is the mother of God."*

Pastoral Letter, *Behold Your Mother,* 82

The Church Celebrates
the Feasts of Mary

In parts 1 and 2, we traced Mary's journey of faith and the
Church's journey of faith with Mary. In this third and final
part, we will consider the same themes, but in light of the
worship of the Church.

The public worship of the Church is called liturgy. The
journeying people of God gather together to pray in praise and
thanksgiving and petition and to celebrate the mystery of
Christ. The liturgy is as familiar as the people of a parish
coming together to celebrate the Eucharist on Sunday. It is
the celebration of the sacrament of reconciliation—the
confession of our sins and our meeting with God's merciful
forgiveness. It is bringing the newborn to the parish church to

be baptized. It is the celebration of a wedding. It is the funeral Mass for someone we love. The liturgy follows the rhythm of our lives week by week and at special moments; it identifies us as a journeying people of prayer. Through the sacred liturgy, we meet and enter into the mystery of Jesus Christ in his dying and rising. This holy encounter transforms us individually and as his people.

The liturgy, especially the eucharistic liturgy, has a double edge: It is an act of remembrance and an act of anticipation. The liturgy draws the past and future into the present moment, reminding us of God's great works and of our hope in their fulfillment. It helps us to remember who God *is* for us and that God is *for* us. Through the remembrance of the liturgy, we know that we have our beginning in God's love and that through the life, death, and resurrection of Jesus we belong to God in a new and everlasting covenant. Discouragement and suffering, joy and success, victories and defeats all take on a new meaning, indeed, are transformed when we remember who we are as God's people.

The liturgy is also an act of anticipation, as well as an act of remembrance. We draw strength from looking forward to God's promises and their fulfillment. People without hope have no future, and people without a future have no life. We have a hope, a future, and life; and the liturgy make these truths real and present to us.

When we understand that remembrance and anticipation are the basic directions of the liturgy, the role of Mary in the worship of the Church comes into clear focus. The Church's journey of faith is a journey of worship with Mary. With her, the Church remembers with gratitude and looks forward in hope to what God has done in Jesus Christ. It is the pattern of her *Magnificat*, her great prayer in Luke's gospel (1:46–55). Mary, the mother of all disciples, takes part in the Church's journey of faith; she therefore participates with the Church worshiping in remembrance and anticipation.

We can now appreciate why the Church celebrates Mary in the liturgy. It celebrates Mary because of who she is in the mystery of Christ and because of what she tells us about this mystery. Jesus' revelation and Mary's faith are intertwined; remembering one recalls the other. She is who she is because of her son, Jesus. He, on the other hand, is the revelation of God in his humanity because of his mother, Mary. We celebrate Mary in the liturgy because the Church sees in her its direction, which takes its origin and finds its completion in Jesus Christ.

The Church's year of worship is arranged in two cycles, or sequences, that are repeated yearly. The first and preeminent cycle is called the temporal cycle. Its central point and primary focus is the Easter Triduum, which includes Holy Thursday, Good Friday, and Holy Saturday–Easter Sunday. These days celebrate the major moments for our journey of faith: the death and the resurrection of Jesus Christ.

The other cycle, which runs at the same time as the temporal cycle, is called the sanctoral cycle. It includes the feast days of Mary and the commemoration of various saints; most of these occur on weekdays. Like the celebrations of the temporal cycle, the feasts of the sanctoral cycle are oriented and directed to the mystery of Christ. They highlight the mystery of Christ in their own way, recalling how it has taken root in the lives of Mary and the saints. We are reminded that they have an intimate relationship with Jesus and that their lives are worthy of imitation.

In this third and final part of the book most of our attention will center on the sanctoral cycle, specifically on seven feasts and solemnities of Mary:

The Immaculate Conception—December 8;

Our Lady of Guadalupe—December 12;

Mary, the Mother of God—January 1;

The Annunciation—March 25;

The Visitation—May 31;

The Assumption—August 15; and

The Birth of Mary—September 8.

For each feast and solemnity, we will first consider the gathering and remembering that occurs in the celebration; in other words, we will try to determine what is celebrated. Our next step will be to identify the sense of gratitude that each feast inspires. The sense of gratitude naturally moves us to praise and thanksgiving. Our third step will be to consider the hope and anticipation involved in the celebration; a feast is an occasion for the Church to look ahead and to renew its hope anchored in faith.

The final step will be to consider the renewed sense of mission that we should carry away from the celebration of a feast. At the end of the Mass, just before we leave the church, we are given a mandate: "Go in peace to love and serve the Lord." We will try to determine how the feasts of Mary renew our sense of mission, how they enable and empower us to move out of the celebration with an awareness of being sent to a waiting world.

The Immaculate Conception

(DECEMBER 8)

What does the Church celebrate when it comes together in worship on the solemnity of the Immaculate Conception? Why does the Church gather and remember on December 8 each year?

A good place to find the answers is in the proclamation of the doctrine in 1854. Pope Pius IX declared: "From the first moment of her conception, the Most Blessed Virgin Mary by a unique grace and privilege of God and in view of the merits of Jesus Christ, the savior of the human race, was preserved from all stain of original sin." We believe that Mary received the effect of her son's life, death, and resurrection from the very first moment of her conception. She never experienced any alienation or distance from God; at her birth, she was already in a loving relationship with him. Later, her unique holiness enabled her to say yes to God's call. Her yes found its origin and power in her unique gift of holiness, in her Immaculate Conception.

Stated this way, the doctrine of the Immaculate Conception might not move us to celebration. This is because we must first allow its message to penetrate our minds and hearts. Once it has done this, we can truly appreciate the doctrine; we might even experience the wonder and awe similar to the reaction of seeing a marvel of nature like the Grand Canyon or a magnificent work of art.

To truly understand the Immaculate Conception is to appreciate the awesome and magnificent dimensions of God's loving involvement in human history. It dramatizes the fact that God's story is intertwined with our story. On the solemnity of the Immaculate Conception, we gather and remember that God's initiative is at the beginning, at the center, and again at the end of our journey of faith. Mary's Immaculate Conception points to the God who begins our story and draws it to completion; he not only called Mary but also prepared her and opened her heart to the possibilities of his love.

If Mary's Immaculate Conception speaks of God's initiative from the very beginning of her life, it also speaks about who we are by God's gift and invitation. On Mary's feast, we gather and remember who we are; she belongs with us in God's journeying family of faith. The celebration of her Immaculate Conception enables us to gather and remember the ways that God has taken initiative in our own lives as well, calling us and preparing us and opening us to the possibilities of his love.

For many, and perhaps most of us, this happened when our parents brought us to the church to be baptized. As children, we were surrounded by an atmosphere of faith, hope, and love; we were opened to possibilities in the future. None of this was a result of our own making. It was given as a gift; God's love was at work from the beginning of our lives. And it is still at work in the voice of other people, in our own sudden and unaccounted for inspirations, and in our accomplishments that time and again seem to exceed our native abilities. We gather and remember Mary's Immaculate Conception; we also gather and remember the graced story of our own lives.

We can speak of a combined celebration taking place on the solemnity of the Immaculate Conception: We celebrate who Mary is through a unique gift of God and who we are by reason of a similar gift. By gathering and remembering, we come to recognize another important fact in our journey of faith: We understand ourselves in Mary and in one another. When we look on Mary, we come to an understanding of ourselves.

Self-knowledge is notoriously difficult to achieve and often occurs when we see ourselves mirrored in other people. Children arrive at a sense of their own identity by seeing themselves in their parents. A husband and wife know themselves in each other. Self-knowledge and self-understanding on the journey of faith occur in a similar way. When we look on one another and on those especially close to God, such as Mary, we come to know ourselves. On the solemnity of the Immaculate Conception, we gather and remember that Mary offers us a possibility for understanding ourselves in God.

The liturgical celebration of the Immaculate Conception means gathering and remembering God's gift of holiness to Mary, a gift that we have also received in our own way. This naturally leads us to praise and thanksgiving. It also involves looking forward in hope. Faith turns into hope when we recognize that what God has already done is only the beginning of what he will do. If God has given the gift, he will surely bring it to completion. Saint Paul spoke of this when he wrote: "I am confident of this, that the one who began a good work among you will bring it to completion by the day of Jesus Christ" (Philippians 1:6).

With hope we have a future to live for. Indeed, we draw life and energy and courage from the future. If we have nothing to look forward to, we wither and die. If we have a future, we live. Since the celebration of the Immaculate Conception opens our eyes to God's gift at work in Mary and ourselves, we have a cause for hope. God is faithful; once he gives a gift he brings it to fulfillment.

At the end of Mass, we are sent out as a changed people and with a mission or purpose. We are empowered and commissioned to discover God's gift in our own lives and in the lives of other people. This requires being attentive to the common and ordinary things in life that often go by unnoticed. In our breath and our pulse, in the accomplishments of our ordinary work, in the beauty of art and music, in the sounds and smells of nature, in the tears and laughter of our friends and children, we find that God's gift invades every corner, every moment of our lives. And although life is marked with the ambiguous signs of sin and evil and death, the attentive and discerning person discovers the deeper reality of God's gift beneath these signs.

The solemnity of the Immaculate Conception as it is celebrated by the journeying people of faith echoes Mary's prayer when she proclaimed: "For the Mighty One has done great things for me, and holy is his name" (Luke 1:49).

Our Lady of Guadalupe, Patroness of the Americas

(DECEMBER 12)

The feast of Our Lady of Guadalupe commemorates the appearances of Mary to Blessed Juan Diego, a poor Aztec Indian man, that took place in 1531 at Tepeyac hill, just north of Mexico City. The apparitions occurred at a time when life was especially difficult for the Indians. Ten years earlier in 1521, Spain had conquered Mexico. The new conquerors exploited the country for its wealth and this naturally led to the oppression of the native population. Greed became a driving force.

Many dedicated missioners went to Mexico from Spain. They hoped to bring Christianity to the Indians of Mexico, but their zealous efforts brought few results—there were not very many conversions to Christianity. One reason was that the Indians found a contradiction between the teaching of the missioners and the greed and oppression of the conquistadors. Nothing hampered the missionary efforts as much as the apparent lack of Christian values among the conquerors.

Another reason was that the Indians felt the humiliation of being a conquered people under the control of the Spanish. It was not likely that they would readily embrace the religion of those who had taken over their country. It should also be remembered that the Indians of Mexico had their own religion. Their deeply rooted Aztec religion, based on symbols that linked the people with the earth, sun, and moon, could not be displaced easily by Christianity.

The story of Juan Diego includes several apparitions of Mary in the course of a few days. The first occurred as he was going to church on December 9, 1531, the date for the solemnity of the Immaculate Conception at the time. He heard music and the voice of a woman speaking his native language, Nahuatl. She identified herself as Mary, the Mother of God, and requested that Juan Diego go to Bishop Zumarraga, the bishop of Mexico, to tell him that she wanted a church built on Tepeyac hill.

The bishop was reluctant to believe him, but indicated that he would accept the message if the Lady of Tepeyac gave some sign. After Juan Diego explained this condition to Mary, she told him to gather the roses that had grown out of season on the hill. He gathered them, and she helped arrange them in his *tilma*, a large cloak used like an apron. When Juan Diego let the roses fall to the floor before the bishop, he wondered why the bishop did not seem to notice them. Instead, the bishop kept staring intently at the *tilma*. Then he looked down and saw the image of Mary painted on it. This image is still venerated in Mexico today and is known throughout the world.

It is important to study the details of this beautiful image. Mary is a young *mestiza*, a woman of mixed blood, readily identifiable as one of the poor and conquered people of Mexico. Even the clothes she is wearing make her one with them. Recall that Mary spoke to Juan Diego in Nahuatl, the native Aztec language, not in Spanish, the language of the conquerors. Because she was one with the people in her appearance, clothing, and language, she was also one with them in their suffering and oppression.

The details of the image give another message to those familiar with Aztec beliefs. Since Mary is standing in front of the sun, just allowing its rays to radiate around her, her position signified that she was more powerful than the Aztec sun god. Since she is standing on top of the moon, her position signified that she was more powerful than the moon god. Of course, Mary herself is not a goddess. This is evident from the position of her head: It is bowed in humility and in recognition of one greater than herself. The image is also an invitation to accept Christianity—Mary is wearing the band worn by pregnant women; she awaits her child, the one whom she offers to her people.

Mary, as Our Lady of Guadalupe, identifies with the poor, the suffering, and the oppressed. Throughout history, she has identified with all people whose dreams are broken, whose hopes are crushed. In her own journey of faith, Mary stood at the foot of the cross. She knew pain, suffering, and oppression as well as she knew her son. She is one with us as we stand before the mystery of the cross in whatever shape it takes in our lives: In physical pain or with a broken spirit or deep sense of loss. Because she has identified so thoroughly with suffering, because she was a woman of faith who hoped against hope, Mary is venerated under special titles, such as Our Lady of Sorrows and Sorrowful Mother.

Under the title of our Lady of Guadalupe, Mary identifies herself with the poor, the suffering, and the oppressed in the

New World. She not only identified with the conquered people of Mexico in their suffering, she also identified with them in all aspects of their life. She was one with the people as a *mestiza*. She was one with them in the symbols of their culture and language and in an appreciation of their religious traditions. This complete identification with the people had its effect on the work of the missioners.

After the story of Juan Diego was told, the conversion rate among the Mexican people increased to an astonishing degree. The increase was so dramatic that it has been called miraculous. Christianity was no longer seen as a foreign religion brought into Mexico from the outside. Through Our Lady of Guadalupe, Christianity appeared to be a genuine option for the Mexican people. Rather than being something imposed from without, Christianity seemed to spring from the culture and religious traditions of the people themselves.

Our Lady of Guadalupe could be seen, in fact, as a rallying point at a time when the Mexican people sought to come to terms with their situation. She represented the victorious presence of God in the midst of a conquered and oppressed people. Pope John Paul II has highlighted Mary's role in evangelization. He wrote: "The appearance of Mary to the native Juan Diego . . . had a decisive effect on evangelization. Its influence greatly overflows the boundaries of Mexico, spreading to the whole continent. America, which historically has been, and still is, a melting-pot of peoples, has recognized in the *mestiza* face of the Virgin of Tepeyac, 'in Blessed Mary of Guadalupe, an impressive example of perfectly inculturated evangelization' " (*Ecclesia in America*, 11).

In other places, too, Mary has drawn together the experience of a people and a sense of the presence of God. For many centuries, Mary has been a rallying point for the Polish people. As Our Lady of Czestochowa, Queen of Poland, she affirms the independence of the Polish people; they have always belonged to themselves and to their God, and not to any conquering or occupying forces. So, too, our Lady of Guadalupe brings the people of Mexico together in a sense of their oneness and dignity and in a sense of the presence of God among them.

The liturgical celebration of this feast recalls what happened for the people of Mexico and the Americas, as well as for believers throughout the world. Mary as Our Lady of Guadalupe is a sign that God identifies with his people, especially the poor; our God is not a distant God, an absentee landlord who keeps accounts. The God revealed in Mary's apparitions as Our Lady of Guadalupe intensely loves his people. God's saving love moves into the history and circumstances and culture of a people. The journey of faith with Mary does not take us into a foreign or alien land. We are already traveling in our home country when we journey in faith.

The gathering and remembering on Mary's feast of Our Lady of Guadalupe leads us to praise and thanksgiving. It is natural to think of God and his presence as real, but not immediate, to our lives. How could the Lord of glory, the Creator of the world, be involved in the human situation and in our struggles? Yet this is precisely the God who is encountered in the feast of Our Lady of Guadalupe.

God is close to his people and moves from within their situations and cultures and ways of life. This closeness and this movement from within are as clear as the presence of Our Lady of Guadalupe was to Juan Diego and the Mexican people. This is good news of a great gift, leading us to praise God and thank him in this feast.

The liturgy of Our Lady of Guadalupe celebrates what God has done and who God is for us. It not only leads us to praise and thanksgiving, it also points us in a future direction. The feast enables us to look ahead with hope. If the feast of Our Lady of Guadalupe recalls the close ways that God has been and is present to his people, then it also signals the way that God will be present to his people. The feast enables us to hope in the continued presence of God in our life and history.

Our hope is rooted in our faith in Jesus Christ, the incarnate word of God. John's gospel captures the power of the incarnation in the very first chapter: "And the Word became flesh and lived among us" (John 1: 14). A literal translation of the original Greek would make the impact of the verse even more dramatic: "The Word became flesh and pitched his tent among us." God has joined us.

When theologians speak of God's immanence, they refer to the intimacy of God's presence to us. God does indeed dwell with his people. This is our assurance that he will not forget us, that he will not abandon us. The Lord speaking through the prophet Isaiah said: "Can a woman forget her nursing child, or show no compassion for the child of her womb? Even these may forget, yet I will not forget you. See, I have inscribed you on the palms of my hands. . ." (Isaiah 49:15–16).

Perhaps in these words of Isaiah we get a glimpse of the power of Our Lady of Guadalupe. She represents the faithful and loving presence of God, especially to those who suffer and feel oppression and need to be reminded of God's faithfulness. In Mary and with Mary, we are in touch with the human ways of God so pointedly that we can never forget his presence, a presence that gives foundation to our hope for the future and to our present mission.

We are also strengthened for our mission. God is close to his people and continues to show this closeness through ordinary channels. Just as Juan Diego's mission was to announce the closeness of God to his people through the apparitions of Mary, so too we are sent to announce and manifest God's presence. The feast of Our Lady of Guadalupe is a powerful reminder that God makes his presence in the world felt through us. We are responsible for continuing the mission of evangelization with Mary and in the pattern of her example.

Mary, the Mother of God

(JANUARY 1)

The Solemnity of Mary, Mother of God, occurs at the beginning of the calendar year and in the middle of the Christmas season. It invites us to renew ourselves in the mystery of Christ. In professing and celebrating Mary as the virgin Mother of God, we remember and acknowledge the unity of the person of Jesus Christ, the Word made flesh, who is both divine and human. We remember and acknowledge that he was conceived by the power of the Holy Spirit. He is from God and for us. We also acknowledge Mary's special relationship to Jesus and its implication for our journey of faith.

In order to understand the full meaning of Mary's relationship to Jesus, we have to consider her motherhood. As mother, Mary conceived and gave birth to Jesus. In the striking words of the Eastern Church, she was the "womb of God." Her motherhood, of course, did not stop with the birth of Jesus. She tenderly held him out and presented him to the world as the first evangelizer. The gospels have her holding her child before the shepherds, who represented the poor and waiting people of Israel. She also held her child before the Magi, who came to pay him homage as representatives of the Gentile world. This motherly action has stirred the imagination of believers over the centuries. Many icons, paintings of the Eastern Church, represent her holding her child toward believers. Western art has also found a constant source of inspiration in the theme of the Madonna and child.

Mary held her son. She did what every mother does. She fed her child and attended to his physical needs. She watched him grow up. She also provided him with the emotional support and love that contributed to the full development of his humanity. Then at a certain point, she faced the hardest part of being a mother. She had to let him go. She had to surrender him and allow him to become who he was destined to become.

Every mother who faces an empty house after the children have gone to school or after they have married knows the price of loving one's children. Mary as mother let go of Jesus in her own unique way. She surrendered him to his public ministry; she let go again at the cross.

The moments of Mary's motherhood reflect in some way the relationship between every mother and child, but for Mary they take on a startling meaning. Her relationship with Jesus was a relationship with God. Jesus was the son of Mary, but he was also the Son of God. The joys, the worries, the anxieties, and the hopes that go into being a mother were the elements of her relationship with God in her son, Jesus. On the Solemnity of Mary, Mother of God, we celebrate her intimate relationship with God. She gives us a dramatic example of the possibilities for our own relationship with him.

As we recognize the immensity of God's gift, which Mary reflects, we are moved to praise and thanksgiving. One could think of God as someone who is loving but remote, a God who really does not need us. Our celebration of Mary as the Mother of God, however, is a challenge to thoughts about that kind of God. Through Mary, God has become deeply involved with us; this is reflected in the intimacy of the mother-child relationship between Mary and Jesus. Our reaction should accordingly be one of wonder and amazement.

As we contemplate and celebrate Mary, the Mother of God, we can only wonder at the extent of God's love in the incarnation: How truly the Word of the Father has taken on our humanity, how real the possibility is for a deep relationship with God. Unimagined possibilities unfold in our lives; a closeness and an intimacy with God beyond our dreams is possible.

When we celebrate the motherhood of Mary, we recognize her closeness to God in Jesus, her son. We also recognize the possibility of our own close relationship with God. In celebration we look forward in hope. We cling to the relationship with God in Jesus Christ. The truth of our hope, what grounds it as a well-founded hope, is as true for us as it was for Mary: It is our access to divinity in the Word made flesh, that is, our relationship with God in Jesus Christ.

This relationship has its roots in the covenant, or pact, that God made with Abraham (Genesis 17:1–2). God invited Abraham into his friendship. Then at Sinai (Exodus 24:7–8), Moses and the people of Israel were bound to God in another covenant relationship, but the people did not live up to it. So God promised a new covenant: "The days are surely coming, says the LORD, when I will make a new covenant with the house of Israel and the house of Judah. . . . But this is the covenant that I will make with the house of Israel after those days, says the LORD: I will put my law within them, and I will write it on their hearts; and I will be their God, and they shall be my people" (Jeremiah 31:31–33). The birth of Jesus signaled the beginning of this new covenant.

As we celebrate the Solemnity of Mary, Mother of God, we gather and remember and praise and thank and look forward in hope. The celebration of God's intimate relationship with the human family, as it is focused in Mary, the mother of Jesus, also empowers us for our life and mission. The celebration of a covenant relationship involves not only accepting it but also giving a response.

Every deep and significant relationship, every covenant, needs renewal so that it can be kept alive and growing as circumstances change. I recall a couple celebrating their fiftieth wedding anniversary. Asked how they stayed married for so many years, they replied that over the course of their years together they "kept marrying" each other. Just as they kept renewing their covenant to each other, so must we keep renewing our covenant with God.

The recognition and celebration of our intimate covenant relationship with God finds a focus in the Solemnity of Mary, Mother of God. Through the celebration of the feast, we are enabled to keep renewing our relationship with God, to keep responding to his invitation to walk in his presence. In all of this, what draws us forward is God's faithful love.

The Annunciation

(MARCH 25)

Nine months before the celebration of Christmas, the Church celebrates the feast of the Annunciation. On this day, we gather and remember how the power of God was made known in the conception of Jesus, the Word made flesh. The feast celebrates Mary, but in relationship to Jesus, her son. It recalls Mary's yes to God's call. "Mary said, 'Here am I, the servant of the Lord; let it be with me according to your word' " (Luke 1:38).

Mary heard the call of God and accepted her responsibility; she responded freely and generously. On the feast of the Annunciation, we gather and remember Mary as a woman of faith who was open and attentive to the word of God, faithful in responding to that word, and willing to risk herself in a free and generous response. In her freedom and generosity, she gave herself entirely to God: her body, her predictable future, her plans, her feelings. She answered God's call with a singleness of mind and heart, a purity of heart that made her blessed. The feast, then, celebrates God's call and Mary's free response.

On the feast of the Annunciation, we celebrate a deep freedom that belongs to us. At times, especially at times of crisis, we can forget or even deny our freedom. An older person suddenly develops pain, and perhaps some bleeding.

The diagnosis comes and the news is not good: The illness is serious. After some denial and perhaps some anger, the person becomes resigned and says, "There is nothing I can do." The words indicate the underlying feeling: some cruel fate has overtaken me.

A family suffers through the loss of a child. Stunned and crushed at the sudden transformation of vibrant young life into death, they ask, "Why did this have to happen?" Underlying their question is a sense of helplessness, of a senseless destiny that they cannot control. A steelworker with a large family finds himself out of a job because his plant has been closed. Decisions made halfway across the world have cut off the source of his livelihood. He throws up his hands and says, "There is nothing I can do." A dark shadow of fate seems to overtake him: He feels a loss of freedom.

At one time or another, all of us have felt that our lives have been taken out of our control. At times, we feel and even accept the absence of personal freedom. Of course, we are conditioned by family background and environment; our lives are not totally in our control. But the Annunciation proclaims a deep freedom that does belong to us. Our freedom is deep in the sense that the deepest parts of our lives are under our control. We set our own directions.

Mary's life as a young woman living in a poor village in Palestine during the first century was obviously determined by a number of elements. In God's call, however, she experienced her freedom; she set the direction of her life as she exercised her freedom by responding to God's invitation.

There are many things about which we really can do nothing. Nevertheless, we are free. I recall a young family man who was suffering from a chronic disease of the bones. In the most confining circumstances, which limited his physical and social freedom, he said, "I am a father and a believer. I have hope." His presence in the hospital enriched the lives of the staff, his fellow patients, and the chaplains. He shifted the question from "What can I do?" to "Who can I be?" In doing so, he rediscovered his freedom.

Freedom is not absolute, but it is radical and deep. It is radical because it comes alive at the roots of who we are. What a marvelous gift, our freedom. God has made us free; we can choose to answer his call. On the feast of the Annunciation, we offer praise and thanksgiving with Mary as we say with her: "For the Mighty One has done great things for me, and holy is his name" (Luke 1:49).

The feast of the Annunciation is also an occasion to look forward in hope. As we celebrate this feast, we bring not only our past, but also our future. Although we have reflected on this idea before, it is good to reconsider it. Our future is very important. In a very real sense, we are our future. We receive our momentum for living from the tomorrow that draws us ahead. The desperate person lives a half-life, or a very diminished life, because the future has been shut out. The energy for living comes from a sense of destination, from a knowledge that something lies ahead.

The future, however, is not something "out there" awaiting our discovery; it does not just arrive one day. We make the future; we move ourselves into the future. Our reflection on Mary's freedom makes us conscious that the future does not come on its own accord; it comes through a free and graced decision. To hope in the future means to believe in and accept our freedom as a reality and as a gift of God.

As on the other feasts of Mary, so on the feast of the Annunciation we are given a mission and are sent forth as a changed people. We return to the rhythm of life as it is lived from day to day. Even in the face of adversity, sickness, loss of job, financial misfortune—we are free. We are free to decide who we will be, how we will relate to God and to other people. The celebration of the Annunciation enables and empowers us to live by God's gift and to live by our freedom.

The Visitation

(MAY 31)

O n the feast of the Visitation, we gather and remember Mary's visit to her cousin Elizabeth. Mary had already received the message of the angel on the occasion of the annunciation and had given her reply. "Mary said, 'Here am I, the servant of the Lord; let it be with me according to your word.' Then the angel departed from her. In those days Mary set out and went with haste to a Judean town in the hill country, where she entered the house of Zechariah and greeted Elizabeth" (Luke 1:38–40).

Our reflections on Mary's journey of faith show us that the visitation was much more than a visit between cousins. Mary was a woman of the Spirit, a woman upon whom the Spirit had come. It was because she had been impelled by the Spirit of God that she went to visit Elizabeth. Mary visited Elizabeth to serve and to proclaim; she went to help Elizabeth during the last months of her pregnancy, as well as to proclaim what God had done for her. On the feast of the Visitation, we celebrate the great deeds of Mary's journey of faith—service and proclamation.

We also celebrate the service and proclamation that we share with Mary in our own journey of faith. Our service and proclamation, like that of Mary, springs from our faith and experience of God. This is most evident when we find ourselves doing and saying what seems to be beyond our native capacities. Although our service and proclamation may occur in dramatic and extraordinary ways, they are usually woven almost unnoticeably into the fabric of our daily lives. Our service may involve a direct form of care for people, such as the sick. It may be parents' care for their child, their work to support the family, or involvement in community affairs. It may mean issuing a challenge to the larger structures of society that exploit and hurt people.

Our proclamation of what God has done may be public: The preaching of a priest or deacon, the reading of Scripture at Mass by a lector, or giving religious instruction. Our proclamation may also be personal: Offering a word of hope at a wake, giving someone advice, or standing up for justice and reconciliation. Whatever the shape or the form, we, like Mary, serve and proclaim. On the feast of the Visitation, we gather and remember these aspects of our journey of faith. They need to be remembered and celebrated.

It is important to note that Mary's service and proclamation flowed out of her deep personal faith. Service and proclamation that do not have their origins in a true, genuine, and deep faith experience can become propaganda or hollow words and empty deeds. On the other hand, a faith experience that does not inspire service and proclamation remains a merely private affair locked tightly inside the individual believer.

Our earlier reflections on the communion of saints can help us understand the close connection between a personal experience of faith and sharing it with others. As Christians, we are not independent believers, but members of a family of faith on a journey together. The consequences of this shared journey are important. Faith not only places us in a relationship with God, it also puts us in a relationship with one another in the mystery of Christ. This mystery is God's plan to bring all things under the headship of Jesus Christ.

As we gather and remember the ways of faith on the feast of the Visitation, we are also drawn to give thanks and praise. Being touched by God is the story of our lives. He is there in our struggles and triumphs, in our joys and sorrows. We gratefully recognize our call to serve others and to share with them God's good works. We recognize the power of the Spirit within us; the same Spirit enabled and impelled Mary to go forth in service and proclamation. The gift of the Spirit also moves us in the celebration of this feast to praise and thank God, "who is mighty and has done great things for me."

We also experience hope-filled anticipation. We look to a future directed by faith and shaped through service and proclamation. We have an important mission to carry out. To believe in the mission given to each of us individually and as a community is to believe in the future. To believe and to accept this mission is to believe that our part in that future is important. We have been gifted with a call and we have been sent with a purpose. The great things of God in Jesus Christ come alive through our service and proclamation. We may be "just ordinary people," but we make a critical difference in the world. Bringing God's message and sharing his love marks us as a people who must give what we have been given. The ways of service and proclamation are many, but the fundamental direction of our mission is one.

Our mission finds its roots in the mission and ministry of Jesus. According to the gospels, Jesus frequently reflected on his mission. "I came that they may have life, and have it abundantly" (John 10:10b). After the resurrection, he said to his disciples: "As the Father has sent me, so I send you" (John 20:21). We can look forward in hope as we accept our mission to serve and proclaim. We are a part of God's plan to bring all things under the headship of Jesus Christ.

The Assumption
(AUGUST 15)

The solemnity of the Assumption celebrates the doctrine solemnly defined by Pope Pius XII in 1950: "The immaculate and ever-virgin Mary, Mother of God, was assumed body and soul into the glory of heaven when her life on earth was completed." When we reflected on this doctrine in part two, we saw that it is not simply a statement without meaning for our own lives. In the doctrine of the Assumption, we celebrate the power of the risen Lord.

When we celebrate Mary's Assumption, we acknowledge what God has done. We recall that Mary, who belongs to the human family, already enjoys the fullness of life with God. In celebrating what God has done in Mary, we gratefully acknowledge our own hope for our destiny as we surrender our lives into the hands of God. The Assumption is closely tied to our own personal and deep hopes.

In order to appreciate how closely the Assumption is tied to our hopes, we must also see the other side of hope, which is fear. We have to see how the solemnity of the Assumption reverses our fears and worst expectations. We know that one day we will die, and we naturally fear that moment. We also dread the countless ways that our lives begin to "fall apart" through aging, illness, and the like. Great amounts of money and energy are spent on maintaining a youthful appearance. All of these are efforts to rescue ourselves from death.

In the face of this natural human fear, we celebrate the solemnity of the Assumption of Mary, with its roots in the resurrection of Jesus. We affirm that with death life is not ended but merely changed. What we perceive to be the patterns of decline and disintegration in our lives do not have the last word. Beyond them and even within them, there is a power of life that is stronger than any death-dealing forces we might encounter. The power of Jesus' resurrection has already taken hold of Mary; she now enjoys the fullness of life with God. The same power is also at work in us, although its measure is not yet evident. Mary's gift of the fullness of life that she now enjoys belongs to us only in hope. The fears and the pain connected with dying remain, but they are wrapped in hope.

With gratitude we are led to praise and thanksgiving as we celebrate the solemnity of the Assumption. It is also an occasion for renewing our hope, which is anchored in the resurrection of Jesus. Jesus is Lord! He is the risen one, among us even now.

Jesus is Lord! When this profession of faith comes from the heart, it is a double-edged sword that cuts through life and death. It enables us to interpret life and death in light of the resurrection and to affirm that our lives continue in a trans-formed way after death. Our lives go beyond what we perceive as the completion of life on earth. At the same time, we affirm that even now new life, the fullness of life, is breaking into our world.

Beneath the shadows of death-dealing forces and the elements of disintegration, life wells up. It wells up not simply as an impersonal cosmic force, but as the presence of the loving and living God who is the source and destiny of all life. The presence of God is evident in the resurrection of Jesus; its effect shines out in the Assumption of Mary. Its power can be seen in our new way of life. When we love one another in life-giving ways; when we create new possibilities in art, science, or our daily work; when we let hardened relationships thaw out with forgiveness; when we live compassionately, the power of the presence of God's new life can be seen. This is what we celebrate on the solemnity of the Assumption.

We are also enabled to move with new strength and conviction from this celebration into the course of ordinary life. We should come away with a new outlook on life and death and eternal life. We should be able to sort out the fears and possibilities, the losses and the gains of our lives. On the solemnity of the Assumption, we celebrate the power of the risen Lord as it has taken hold in a member of the human family. Mary already enjoys the fullness of life that we look forward to in hope.

The Birth of Mary

(SEPTEMBER 8)

E very journey must have its pauses, times for refreshment and reorientation. As the Church gathers and remembers on the feast of the birth of Mary, it pauses to celebrate its own life and mission. On the feast of the birth of Mary, what the Church is—its life—coincides with what the Church is about—its mission. This feast is a family celebration; the Church's life is the life of a family, and its mission is to draw all people into God's new family of faith.

We surround birthday celebrations with an amazing variety of gimmicks—cards, balloons, hats, gifts, cake, and candles—and rituals: Surprising the birthday person, singing "Happy Birthday," blowing out the candles, and making a wish. The gimmicks and rituals have their point: The family assembles to celebrate its life together by centering its attention on one member of the family. In this one person, the family is able to focus its identity as a unique group of people who laugh and weep with one another, support and love one another.

So, too, the journeying Church gathers on September 8 and celebrates its life as a family of faith. It centers its attention on Mary, the preeminent and unique member of the family. In celebrating Mary's birthday, the Church remembers its identity as a family of faith, a group of people who believe together, pray together, and serve one another and the world.

Mary, a fellow disciple of Jesus and mother of all disciples, provides the occasion for the Church to celebrate its life together.

In this family celebration, the Church also gathers and remembers its mission, what it is about in this world. As it celebrates its life together, it also recalls its mission to draw all people into the family of God. It invites people to come home and belong to the family that has the source of its relationships in Jesus Christ. "And looking at those who sat around him, he said, 'Here are my mother and my brothers! Whoever does the will of God is my brother and sister and mother' " (Mark 3:34–35).

The Church is called to proclaim the good news that we are "no longer strangers and aliens, but you are citizens with the saints and also members of the household of God . . ." (Ephesians 2:19). On the feast of the birth of Mary, the Church gathers and remembers its mission to bring all people into the new family of God.

When we gather and remember on Mary's birthday, we are reminded that God generally works in ordinary ways. It is probably natural to think that God works in a grand style; he is after all the Creator of the universe. In fact, as we gather to celebrate Mary's birthday, we are reminded that God works in very ordinary ways. The gospel for the feast, which traces the genealogy, or human descent of Jesus, celebrates God's presence in close relationships and family ties. What could be more ordinary than that?

Our remembering and gathering and praising and thanking as a family on Mary's birthday directs us to a faith that gives us hope now and in the future. In a renewed way, we believe that God in Jesus Christ has entered and shared our history. Because of the coming of Jesus in the flesh, what we call *our* history is not merely the sum of the parts of our involvement. Our history is a *saving* history. Our story and God's story come together in the same way that the lives of two people who love each other come together in the shared history of marriage. When we grasp how our story is linked with God's story, we have a sure foundation for our hope. We can antic-ipate our fulfillment as a family of faith because our life in God's new family has already begun.

Celebrating the birth of Mary as a family can be a source of strength for our journey and mission. We recognize that we belong to God and to one another, perhaps more closely than we ever dared to imagine. To belong to one another means that we are not alone. To belong to one another means that our lives are intertwined, that we share and receive life from each other. In all of this, we come in touch with a power to live in a new way. It is the power to live closely to God and to one another in faith, hope, and love. This power is rooted in the mystery of Christ, God's plan to bring all things under his headship. It is a power lived out in the journeying family of faith with Mary, who is the mother of Jesus and our mother and sister. As the Church, we pray for, await, serve, and proclaim the reign of God—the completion of his new family.

In a sense, our reflections on Mary's journey have brought us full circle. Together with Mary, we are a hinge and link between promise and fulfillment. In ordinary ways and at dramatic moments, we are with Jesus and Mary in the new family of God. We watch and wait and hold our experience of him in our hearts. Mary's journey of faith and our journey of faith are one journey with Jesus, who changes water into wine, wine into blood, blood into tears, and tears into laughter.

Concluding Meditation

HAIL MARY . . .

We are on a journey of faith. The journey takes us across level green plains or into deep valleys or, sometimes, through dry and empty deserts. Then we turn around or look ahead. You are there. We meet you; we greet you. You are an extraordinary person. In your presence we are reverent, perhaps with heads bowed. But we are also familiar with you. You are, after all, mother and sister and daughter and disciple with us.

FULL OF GRACE . . .

An empty cup is filled up, brimming over. Mary, you are the poor one. You stand with hands upturned. God's grace, God's gift, has filled you. Our own emptiness, our aloneness, our neediness take a different shape when we look on you. The moments when we feel that we have little or nothing change into times of possibility. A path is cleared, a way is made for the Lord to journey within us, to fill us. Before you began to be, before we began to be, the richness of the Lord's mercy flowed into his dream for us.

THE LORD IS WITH YOU . . .

You wait and carry a child within you. You hold and feed and care for your child. You watch your son preach and heal and suffer and die and rise. He is the presence of God with us, Emmanuel. We do not make the journey alone. We look on you and we sense the presence of God within us, around us, among us, at the beginning of the journey, and at its conclusion.

BLESSED ARE YOU AMONG WOMEN . . .

Mary, you live not by the great things you do, but by who you are—hearing the word of God and treasuring it. You live the ordinary course of life in an extraordinary way. So, you are blessed, happy. You turn around our standards for greatness, happiness, and fulfillment. As the poor and lowly servant of the Lord, you are called blessed by all generations. We follow your movement into God, and we must change our plans for greatness and for happiness. Your one great good becomes our one great good—to be with him.

AND BLESSED IS THE FRUIT OF YOUR WOMB, JESUS . . .

The Lord of life is so alive within you that you must give birth to him. You do not simply set him to rest in this world. You hold him up and out. You give the gift of the Blessed One as generously and as freely as he has been given to you. We walk with you. We speak the Word we have heard. We hold and share the Life that fills our hands.

HOLY MARY, MOTHER OF GOD . . .

Mary, you are holy. You are the mother of the Lord. Your holiness and our possibility for holiness are sketched in your eyes. They are eyes that wait and watch, eyes that wonder and observe and attend. They are eyes that weep and laugh.

161

Your eyes speak to us of the holiness of God in human ways, because they constantly look upon Jesus, who is the Holy One of God and our brother in human flesh.

PRAY FOR US SINNERS . . .

We freely ask you to pray for us. How can we not do so? You are with us and among us; you have walked with us and toward us. We are sinners, pilgrims on a journey who stumble and fall and struggle and imperfectly make our way. Your son has touched us and healed us and forgiven us. We can never forget or lose the memory of who we are—people in need of his love.

NOW . . .

Now is the time of our hoping and struggling. Today we hear his voice. We do not want to harden our hearts or dull his presence. Today is the time, and now is the prayer.

AND AT THE HOUR OF OUR DEATH. AMEN.

Mary, we can journey in our life only if we have the food of hope, only if we have some sense of our destination, only if we believe that we can follow your son in his dying and, then, in his rising. Keep us alive and journeying in the memory that Jesus is Lord. He is the risen one who is our life and resurrection. Amen.

A Selection
of Marian Prayers

The Church both in the East and the West has a rich tradition of prayers addressed to Mary. Some of these prayers are part of the fabric of the liturgical or official public prayer of the Church, such as Mary's *Magnificat*, her song of praise drawn from Luke 1:46–55. Other prayers are devotional, the prayers of individuals and groups that express a devoted attachment to and reliance on Mary, Mother of God and Mother of the Church.

The prayers that follow are a selection of mainly devotional prayers, which have engaged the minds and hearts of countless people across generations and cultures and languages. They have been on the lips of our mothers and fathers in faith and have expressed their sense of veneration for and reliance on the Mother of God. May they find a place in our hearts and in our daily lives.

THE HAIL MARY

Hail, Mary, full of grace, the Lord is with you.
Blessed are you among women,
and blessed is the fruit of your womb, Jesus.

Holy Mary, Mother of God,
pray for us sinners,
now and at the hour of our death.
Amen.

THE ROSARY OF
THE BLESSED VIRGIN MARY

The rosary is a simple, powerful, and absorbing way of prayer. In the words of Pope John Paul II, it is a way of contemplating Christ with Mary. (See his apostolic letter *On the Most Holy Rosary,* 2002.)

The rosary begins with the recitation of the Apostles' Creed followed by an Our Father and three Hail Mary's—a kind of prelude to what follows. The rosary consists of units of recited or spoken prayer called decades, that is, an Our Father followed by ten Hail Mary's. While each decade is prayed in a vocal and external way, the mind is directed to meditate internally or to consider a mystery or dimension of the life of Christ and his Mother.

There are four sets of five mysteries that make present to us the Gospel in miniature. They are:

THE JOYFUL MYSTERIES

- The Annunciation
- The Visitation
- The Birth of the Lord
- The Presentation of the Lord in the Temple
- The Finding of the Lord in the Temple

THE MYSTERIES OF LIGHT

- The Baptism of the Lord
- The Self-Manifestation of the Lord at the Wedding Feast of Cana

- Jesus' Proclamation of the Kingdom of God
  and the Call to Conversion
- The Transfiguration
- The Institution of the Eucharist

THE SORROWFUL MYSTERIES

- The Agony in the Garden
- The Scourging at the Pillar
- The Crowning with Thorns
- The Carrying of the Cross
- The Crucifixion and Death of the Lord

THE GLORIOUS MYSTERIES

- The Resurrection
- The Ascension
- The Descent of the Holy Spirit
- The Assumption of the Blessed Virgin Mary
- The Coronation of Mary as Queen of Heaven

THE ANGELUS

The tradition of praying the Angelus is a longstanding and beautiful custom. The Angelus or prayer of the angel's greeting to Mary is prayed early in the morning, at noon, and in the evening. These three points in the day are marked rhythmically by a memory of the mystery of the Incarnation.

Verse: The Angel of the Lord declared unto Mary,
Response: And she conceived of the Holy Spirit
Hail Mary . . .

Verse:	Behold the handmaid of the Lord.
Response:	Be it done unto me according to your word.
	Hail Mary . . .

Verse:	And the Word was made flesh.
Response:	And dwelt among us.
	Hail Mary . . .

| *Verse:* | Pray for us, O holy Mother of God, |
| *Response:* | That we may be made worthy of the promises of Christ. |

Let us pray.
Pour forth, we beg you, O Lord, your grace into our hearts: that we, to whom the Incarnation of Christ your Son was made known by the message of an angel, may by his Passion and Cross be brought to the glory of his Resurrection. Through the same Christ our Lord. Amen.

THE REGINA COELI

During the Easter season, instead of the Angelus, the *Regina Coeli* or Queen of Heaven is prayed.

Queen of heaven, rejoice, alleluia:
For he whom you merited to bear, alleluia,
Has risen, as he said, alleluia.
Pray for us to God, alleluia.

Verse:	Rejoice and be glad, O Virgin Mary, alleluia.
Response:	Because the Lord is truly risen, alleluia.
	Let us pray.

O God, who by the Resurrection of your Son, our Lord Jesus Christ, granted joy to the whole world: grant, we beg you, that through the intercession of the Virgin Mary, his Mother, may we lay hold of the joys of eternal life. Through the same Christ our Lord.
Amen.

THE SALVE REGINA OR HAIL, HOLY QUEEN

This prayer is recited at the end of the day. It is also appropriately prayed at a time of farewell, such as a wake or funeral.

Hail, holy Queen, Mother of mercy;
hail our life, our sweetness and our hope.
To you do we cry, poor banished children of Eve.
To you do we send up our sighs,
mourning and weeping in this valley of tears.
Turn then, most gracious Advocate,
your eyes of mercy toward us.
And after this our exile show unto us
the blessed fruit of your womb, Jesus.
O clement, O loving, O sweet Virgin Mary.

Verse: Pray for us, Holy Mother of God;
Response: That we may be made worthy of the promises of Christ.

THE MEMORARE

This prayer is a traditional expression of trust and hope in the intercessory power of Mary, especially in times and circumstances of great need.

Remember, O most gracious Virgin Mary,
that never was it known
that anyone who fled to your protection,
implored your help or sought your intercession,
was left unaided.

Inspired by this confidence, I fly to you,
O Virgin of Virgins, my mother.
To you I come;
before you I stand, sinful and sorrowful.
O Mother of the Word Incarnate,
despise not my petitions,
but in your mercy, hear and answer me.
Amen.

LITANY OF THE BLESSED VIRGIN MARY

Lord, have mercy.
> *Lord, have mercy.*

Christ, have mercy.
> *Christ, have mercy.*

Lord, have mercy.
> *Lord, have mercy.*

Christ, hear us.
> *Christ, graciously hear us.*

God the Father of Heaven,
> *have mercy on us* (repeat).

God the Son, Redeemer of the world,
God the Holy Spirit,
Holy Trinity, one God,

Holy Mary,
    pray for us (repeat).
Holy Mother of God,
Holy Virgin of virgins,
Mother of Christ,
Mother of the Church,
Mother of divine grace,
Mother most pure,
Mother most chaste,
Mother inviolate,
Mother undefiled,
Mother immaculate,
Mother most amiable,
Mother most admirable,
Mother of good counsel,
Mother of our Creator,
Mother of our Savior,
Virgin most prudent,
Virgin most venerable,
Virgin most renowned,
Virgin most powerful,
Virgin most merciful,
Virgin most faithful,
Mirror of justice,
Seat of wisdom,
Cause of our joy,
Spiritual vessel,
Vessel of honor,
Singular vessel of devotion,
Mystical rose,
Tower of David,
Tower of ivory,

House of gold,
Ark of the covenant,
Gate of heaven,
Morning star,
Health of the sick,
Refuge of sinners,
Comfort of the afflicted,
Help of Christians,
Queen of angels,
Queen of patriarchs,
Queen of prophets,
Queen of apostles,
Queen of martyrs,
Queen of confessors,
Queen of virgins,
Queen of all saints,
Queen conceived without original sin,
Queen assumed into heaven,
Queen of the most holy rosary,
Queen of families,
Queen of peace,

Lamb of God, who take away the sins of the world,
    spare us, O Lord!

Lamb of God, who take away the sins of the world,
    graciously hear us, O Lord!

Lamb of God, who take away the sins of the world,
    have mercy on us.

Verse: Pray for us, O holy Mother of God.

Response: That we may be made worthy of the promises of Christ.

Let us pray.

Grant, we beg you, O Lord God, that we your servants, may enjoy lasting health of mind and body, and by the glorious intercession of the Blessed Mary, ever Virgin, be delivered from present sorrow and enter into the joy of eternal happiness. Through Christ our Lord.

Response: Amen.

A SELECT BIBLIOGRAPHY
FOR FURTHER STUDY

Pope John Paul II. *Redemptoris Mater (On the Blessed Virgin Mary in the Life of the Church.* Delivered at St. Peter's Basilica in Rome on March 25, 1987, Feast of the Annunciation. (See www.cin.org.)

Pope John Paul II. *Rosarium Virginis Mariae (On the Most Holy Rosary).* Apostolic letter from the Vatican on October 16, 2002, beginning the twenty-fifth year of his pontificate. (See www.newadvent.org.)

Pope Paul VI. *Marialis cultus (For the Right Ordering and Development of Devotion to the Blessed Virgin Mary,* Delivered at S. Peter's in Rome on February 2, 1974, Feast of the Presentation. (See www.cin.org)

Pope Paul VI. *Lumen gentium (Dogmatic Constitution on the Church* of the Second Vatican Council). Chapter VIII, "On the Blessed Virgin Mary, Mother of God in the Mystery of Christ and the Church." Promulgated on November 21, 1964. (See www.vatican.va/archive/)

United States Conference of Catholic Bishops. *Behold Your Mother, Woman of Faith.* 1973. *Pastoral Letters of the United States Catholic Bishops,* Volume III, 1962–1974. (See www.nccbuscc.org)

SCRIPTURE INDEX

Old Testament

Genesis
- 12:1 — *39*
- 17:1–2 — *143*
- 71:4, 7 — *17*

Exodus
- 24:7–8 — *143*

Psalms
- 25:4 — *22*
- 28:2 — *22*
- 62:5–6 — *22*
- 136:1 — *22*

Isaiah
- 49:15–16 — *139*
- 55:8–9 — *91*

Jeremiah
- 31:31–33 — *143–144*

Ezekiel
- 36:28b — *46*

New Testament

Matthew
- 1:18–25 — *31*
- 2:2 — *43*
- 2:11b–12 — *43*
- 6:25 — *26*
- 13:33 — *53*
- 13:44–46 — *34*

Mark
- 1:2 — *25*
- 1:14–15 — *64–65*
- 3:31–34 — *58*
- 3:34 — *59*
- 3:34–35 — *157*
- 3:35 — *60*
- 8:34b–35 — *71*

Luke
- 1:26–38 — *27*
- 1:28 — *100*
- 1:38 — *25, 32, 34, 59, 145*
- 1:38–40 — *149*
- 1:39–49 — *35*
- 1:45 — *39, 69*
- 1:46–55 — *127*
- 1:49 — *133, 147*
- 1:54–55 — *17, 70*
- 2:4–5 — *38*
- 2:7 — *42*
- 2:22–24 — *46*
- 2:34–35 — *47*
- 2:38 — *47*
- 2:40 — *21*
- 2:43–50 — *47–48*
- 2:51 — *49, 86, 99*
- 2:51–52 — *51*
- 4:16–21 — *64*
- 5:11 — *34*
- 6:20b — *52*
- 9:25 — *52*
- 9:51 — *41*
- 9:57–62 — *60*

John
- 1:14 — *92, 139*
- 2:1–11 — *56*
- 2:3b — *57*
- 2:5b — *57*
- 3:16 — *68*
- 10:10b — *152*
- 12:24 — *70*

John	14:12–13	*109*	2 Corinthians	1:20	*18, 101*
	19:25–27	*69*	Galatians	4:4	*91, 92*
	20:21	*152*	Ephesians	1:9–10	*83*
Acts of the				2:19	*105, 157*
Apostles	1:14	*77*	Philippians	1:6	*133*
	2:1–4	*77*	Colossians	3:3	*20*
	10:36–39	*63*	1 Timothy	2:5	*107*
Romans	1:3–4	*73*	Hebrews	1:1–2	*116*
	7:15	*96*		11:8	*39*
	8:29	*73*			
1 Corinthians	12:12, 26	*106*			
	15:35, 42–44	*102*			